Praise for *The Lost Art of Real Cooking*

"*The Lost Art of Real Cooking* wins my vote as the funniest, most eclectic, and most exotic collection of recipes to have been published in a century or more. The exuberance of Ken Albala and Rosanna Nafziger, as they tackle everything from tomato sauce to pecan pie, is quite simply infectious. A lot of these arts, often amusingly described, are indeed lost and deserve to be brought back—harvesting garden snails for instance, brewing beer, catching yeast for sourdough, making ghee, or composing a genuine, old-fashioned, authentic strawberry shortcake. At the same time, the book is a great adjunct to any exercises in culinary history. Once you've followed their directions and incubated your own *koji* mold, Japanese cuisine will never look the same!"

—Nancy Harmon Jenkins, food writer and author of *The New Mediterranean Diet Cookbook*

"This is a real cookery book. The authors share their knowledge, expertise, and philosophy of food all with a sense of humor. They firmly believe that cooking is a pleasure and encourage us to relax and savor the task of preparing what we eat. Ken and Rosanna have a refreshingly old-fashioned approach to cooking and, though I'm keeping my electrical appliances, I can't wait to get pickling, brewing, and cooking my own snails."

—Jennifer McLagan, author of *Fat* and *Bones*

"*The Lost Art of Real Cooking* is a joy to read straight through, like a novel that maps a lost kingdom. Here all foods are real and everyone knows how to make them. Here food is neither lab science nor professional chef-ery. It's homemade craft and everyone is invited to join in the fun. Whether the action is to catch yeast for a sourdough, knead butter from cultured cream, grow mold for miso, cure olives or lemons or pork, make cottage beer or almond milk—this is action-packed daily life as it can be lived. Ken and Rosanna show us how with such gusto that they turn living into an art as real as cooking."

—Betty Fussell, author of *Raising Steaks*

"*The Lost Art of Real Cooking* is a refreshing gem. In a world where gadgets and high-tech techniques seem to rule, *Lost Art* inspires to cook from the heart and soul—food is living and breathing, and the passion and thought we put into our meals does not need to be so measured and calculated. Ken and Rosanna remind us that tradition and intuition need to be kept alive if we are to preserve our culinary heritage for future generations."

—Sam Mogannam, managing partner of the Bi-Rite Family of Businesses in San Francisco

"Traditional techniques and old recipes are just as valuable today. Nobody could be better than Ken Albala and Rosanna Nafziger at evoking the time-honored food of the past."

—Anne Willan, founder of La Varenne Cooking School

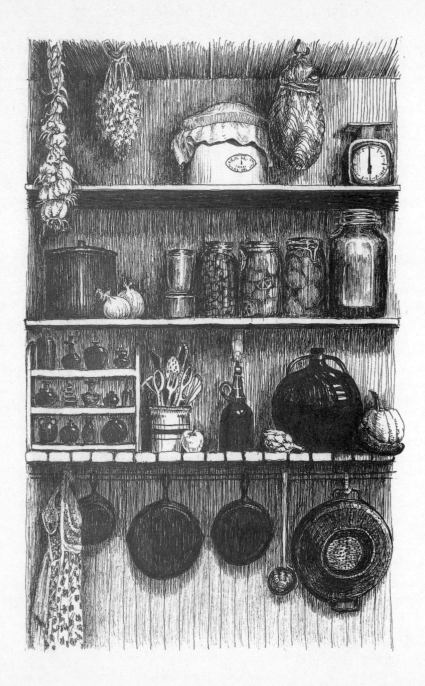

The Lost Art *of* Real Cooking

Rediscovering the Pleasures
of Traditional Food
One Recipe at a Time

AN INTRODUCTION TO THE ANTIQUATED KITCHEN, OR
COOKERY MADE DIFFICULT AND INCONVENIENT BEING
FOREMOST A PLEASANT DISCOURSE ON THE NATURE
AND EXECUTION OF ARCANE AND DANGEROUS CULINARY
PRACTICES ESPECIALLY DESIGNED FOR PATIENT,
DISCERNING INDIVIDUALS WHO APPRECIATE SUPERIOR
HOMEMADE FOOD AND THOSE WHO WILL NOT BALK AT
DEVOTING MANY LABORIOUS HOURS TO THE KITCHEN

KEN ALBALA and ROSANNA NAFZIGER

Illustrations by Marjorie Nafziger

A PERIGEE BOOK

A PERIGEE BOOK
Published by the Penguin Group
Penguin Group (USA) Inc.
375 Hudson Street, New York, New York 10014, USA
Penguin Group (Canada), 90 Eglinton Avenue East, Suite 700, Toronto, Ontario M4P
2Y3, Canada (a division of Pearson Penguin Canada Inc.) • Penguin Books Ltd., 80 Strand,
London WC2R 0RL, England • Penguin Group Ireland, 25 St. Stephen's Green, Dublin 2,
Ireland (a division of Penguin Books Ltd.) • Penguin Group (Australia), 250 Camberwell
Road, Camberwell, Victoria 3124, Australia (a division of Pearson Australia Group Pty. Ltd.)
• Penguin Books India Pvt. Ltd., 11 Community Centre, Panchsheel Park, New Delhi—
110 017, India • Penguin Group (NZ), 67 Apollo Drive, Rosedale, North Shore 0632, New
Zealand (a division of Pearson New Zealand Ltd.) • Penguin Books (South Africa) (Pty.)
Ltd., 24 Sturdee Avenue, Rosebank, Johannesburg 2196, South Africa
Penguin Books Ltd., Registered Offices: 80 Strand, London WC2R 0RL, England

While the author has made every effort to provide accurate telephone numbers and
Internet addresses at the time of publication, neither the publisher nor the author
assumes any responsibility for errors, or for changes that occur after publication.
Further, the publisher does not have any control over and does not assume any
responsibility for author or third-party websites or their content.

First edition: July 2010

Albala, Ken, 1964–
  The lost art of real cooking : rediscovering the pleasures of traditional food one recipe
at a time / Ken Albala and Rosanna Nafziger ; illustrations by Marjorie Nafziger.
      p.   cm.
  "An introduction to the antiquated kitchen, or cookery made difficult and inconvenient
being foremost a pleasant discourse on the nature and execution of arcane and dangerous
culinary practices especially designed for patient, discerning individuals who appreciate
superior homemade food and those who will not balk at devoting many laborious hours
to the kitchen."
  Includes bibliographical references and index.
  ISBN 978-0-399-53588-8
  1. Cookery. 2. Cookery, International. 3. Cookery—History. 4. Cookery—Humor.
5. Food—Preservation—History. I. Nafziger, Rosanna. II. Title.
  TX714.A423 2010
  641.5—dc22   2009047640

PRINTED IN THE UNITED STATES OF AMERICA
10 9 8 7 6 5 4 3 2 1

The recipes contained in this book are to be followed exactly as written. The publisher is not
responsible for your specific health or allergy needs that may require medical supervision.
The publisher is not responsible for any adverse reactions to the recipes contained in this
book.

Most Perigee books are available at special quantity discounts for bulk purchases for sales
promotions, premiums, fund-raising, or educational use. Special books, or book excerpts,
can also be created to fit specific needs. For details, write: Special Markets, Penguin Group
(USA) Inc., 375 Hudson Street, New York, New York 10014.

Contents

Dear Gentle Reader,

It's time to take back the kitchen. It's time to unlock the pantry, to venture once again into our cellars and storehouses, and break free from the golden shackles of convenient, ready-made, industrial food. It's time to cook supper.

Have no fear. Whether you were raised on boxed mac 'n' cheese or suckled by a vending machine, you can learn to fend for yourself in the kitchen. Yes, this book is obstinately old-fashioned, but we recognize that most of us are not yet lucky enough to have a heifer in the backyard. And so we have translated the scale of old barns and wine cellars and bustling bakeries to that of the everyday kitchen. Your kitchen.

The premise of this book is a simple one. For the past half century, Americans have been convinced that cooking is drudgery, an odious task to be avoided at any cost, so that time might be freed up to do other more Important things. We were enticed with a constant stream of ingenious gadgets meant to make our lives easier, as well as products cheerfully advertised as being Quick, Convenient, and Simple to prepare. For the sake of saving labor, these new products were highly processed, packed with artificial flavors and additives, and were usually seriously lacking in the single most indispensable attribute of gastronomic pleasure: Honest Good Taste. Or they were so loaded with sugar and flavor enhancers that our palates eventually became jaded, to the point that we came to prefer powdered fluorescent drinks over real juice, flaccid canned vegetables over briskly crunchy fresh greens, even heinous atrocities such as margarine over real butter. Most important, these industrially produced foods were neither fun to prepare nor interesting to serve. And what did we do with all that free time? We worked longer hours in the office, and came home to work out on our basement treadmills. When you think of it, what could be more important than feeding yourself and others with good, wholesome, well-prepared food and truly enjoying the experience?

Selling food through convenience was, in nearly all respects, a devious deception. Whoever dreamt up the preposterous idea that cooking is no fun has probably never done it. So before you continue, Gentle Reader, if you cannot abide by long hours in the kitchen, this is no book for you. If your idea of cooking is opening up cans and frozen packets, then please do move on. We know there are many cookbooks that cater to such tastes, and that some people are truly strapped for time or simply hate to cook. Rest assured, such people will find nothing diverting herein. We intend to make the process of cooking as long, difficult, and arduous as possible—for a few very simple reasons. Cooking slowly with patience is inherently entertaining, and the food it yields tastes better, costs less, and connects you with the people you feed in a way that a prefabricated meal can never hope to do. There is, it cannot be denied, unspeakable pleasure in providing sustenance for others with the labor of one's own hands.

We intend to cut no corners, use no labor-saving devices or modern equipment, unless in the absolute interest of safety. A good sharp kitchen knife will always be preferred to a processor, a whisk to a stand-up mixer, a brazen flame to an electric appliance whenever feasible. Yes, this will be hard work. But can you see the irony of people who save time and energy with electric gadgets and then traipse off to burn calories at the gym? Why not boldly brandish a whisk instead? Your egg whites will be all the more happy for it, as well as your biceps.

There are other motives in offering you this work. We have both long bemoaned the dumbing-down of cookbooks, the painstaking detail over the simplest of procedures stemming from the assumption that readers know absolutely nothing about cooking. Worse yet is the conversion of recipes over the last century from homey inviting instructions to quasi-scientific experiments, which the reader is warned must be followed with measured precision if anything approaching passable results are to be attained. This book is an effort to loosen up. Cooking is not a science. And dictating strict recipes really teaches aspiring cooks very little, apart from a slavish obedience to directions. We are not averse to measurements per se, they are often necessary, particularly with baking. But to insist that a quarter teaspoon of some particular seasoning is correct while anything more or less, or, heaven forfend, a substitution, altogether amounts to culinary heresy, this is just too much to bear. We invite readers to wander off on their own in the kitchen, be creative and inventive, even spontaneous, and if an exact measurement is necessary, we will gladly offer it. Otherwise, we will humbly suggest a pinch of this, a dab of that, to taste, as we trust very well, Gentle Reader—you actually know what you like best. We equally eschew serving sizes; clearly any recipe ought to be so adaptable as to feed however many are present without the use of a calculator.

This book is also decidedly—no, stubbornly—antiquated. We use fresh fruits and vegetables whenever in season, but also dried, fermented, preserved foods out of season, just as did our forebears. We prefer local food, especially buying it from trusted farmers, but we know very well people in the past used imported spices, ate tropical fruits, drank coffee grown halfway around the world, and many other items that must perforce be grown elsewhere. Being antiquated is not tantamount to going local. Herein we herald a new old-fashioned approach to food—the laborious, inconvenient, difficult, and most important, extraordinarily rewarding nature of food treated with reverence, awe, and respect. This is not merely slowing down to appreciate good traditional food. This book will show you why it is important to spend several weeks making your own sauerkraut and pickles, how curing olives at home takes no complex chemistry but requires immense patience and yields something infinitely finer than those bought in the store. We will discourse on the ancient mysteries of capturing sourdough yeast and culturing butter, the beauty of dismembering haunches of meat and roasting them over an open flame, making serious aged cheese, and watching fruit juice naturally ferment into wine. These were all practices once undertaken by the family, in the home, rather than a factory. These are not high-priced items that need to be imported at great expense. Nor are they threatened artisanal treasures that must be rescued by marketing them in pricy gourmet shops. Recipes here can all be made in the smallest of kitchens without expensive equipment, capturing flavors that speak of place and reflect the labor that rewards only through the sweat of one's brow.

Most important, this book is for beginners, those who never grew up on a farm, but have the longing need to connect on a deeper level with what goes into their bodies. These are skills that a century and a half ago most Americans understood well. They devoted arduous days to making food because it was the way to survive. Today, we seek a different way to survive—by rejecting the indignities imposed on us by industrial food corporations, by daring to make food ourselves when scientists and nutritionists warn us that the industry knows best. We now realize what we have sacrificed in terms of health, happiness, and aesthetic gratification by trusting them. It is time—not to literally turn back the clock, but to reclaim our food heritage. To proudly eat and drink food difficult to prepare because we now know it is worth it, to benefit our bodies, our souls, and the health of our planet and its inhabitants.

The recipes that follow are all drawn from the experience of the authors in the year or so preceding publication. Ours is an odd and fortuitous partnership. We met by accident, struck up an immediate friendship, and realized that our talents complemented each other's but in many ways aimed in different directions. What better excuse to collaborate? All of our projects took place independently (with the exception of a roasted bear's butt) and thus the recipes and stories are attributed carefully, and you will note that we have quite different voices. It seemed better to preserve the quirks of our styles rather than efface our individual personalities.

It is also important to point out that we are indebted to numerous other works, some by experts, others by inveterate dabblers like ourselves. These are all listed in the bibliography. No recipe here replicates what was found elsewhere, but we do think it important to note that some basic procedures were influenced directly by our readings. For example, we only discovered Sandor Katz, a true kindred spirit, after writing most of the sections on fermentation. We were, of course, overjoyed that we hadn't steered off course, and that there were other antiquated souls out there who like to wing it. In any case, the material here directly reflects food we cooked ourselves in our kitchens following our own experience, instinct, and, in some cases, some really old cookbooks.

A NOTE ON RECIPE FORMAT

When the Boston Cooking School developed its ingredients-first recipe system a century ago, it was revolutionary, systematic, and standardized. It made sense for the newly industrialized cooks it served.

As a 12-year-old in the kitchen, however, it baffled Rosanna. She was forever scanning back and forth between ingredients and instructions. *Beat the eggs.* How many eggs? Okay, three eggs. Now where were we? Ah, yes, sugar. In fact, she got so frustrated she rewrote every recipe she made, putting it on an index card as one solid, uninterrupted paragraph of instructions. Beat three eggs. Whisk in one cup sugar. In an old-fashioned kitchen, it made perfect sense.

Why? In the Boston Cooking School method, there is an underlying assumption that the first step in every recipe is to go out and procure all the necessary ingredients and put them in one spot: It's the professional cook's *mise-en-place*, with everything pre-measured and ready to go. Again, that's fine for cakes (if you can hire a dishwasher to wash all those bowls used for said pre-measured ingredients). Most cookery is much more flexible than all that. Ingredients can vary significantly in potency and composition, and sometimes you're better off measuring with your senses than a scale. How does the dough feel? Does the sauerkraut smell right? How does the soup taste?

Furthermore, many of our old-fashioned recipes span the course of *days*, if not *months*. They are not the sort of thing you can assemble in one spot, eat, and have done with. We are cooking all the time—when we feed the starter, peek at the pickles, sniff the peaches to check on their ripeness.

On the flipside, before the Boston Cooking School, cookbooks were much too spare in their instructions. Cookbook writers could assume their readers had vast stores of kitchen lore and experience. A recipe (receipt) wasn't so much a detailed plan for what to do upon entering the kitchen as it was notation that fellow cooks could add to their repertoire. Much like sheet music doesn't tell you how to hold your violin, old-fashioned recipes don't tell you how to cut fat for pastry or knead bread. That's our job, now. As we turn back to the cookery of older centuries, we need old-fashioned recipes with the lore built in—and so we took this narrative approach. We also had to reconstruct many techniques that old cookbooks never mention, either because such knowledge was handed down orally within families, or was dealt with by professionals—as with baking and curing meats, especially in urban settings.

Note also, since we worked independently on this book, we have both signed our own recipes. If you are wondering who is speaking when we mention "I," just look at the end of each recipe section.

A NOTE ON KITCHENS

We have cooked successfully in many kitchens—from highly efficient commercial kitchens to the sort where you have to go outside to get water and kindling, from sunless, cramped urban two-by-four kitchens to steaming-pie-in-the-window-looking-over-rolling-fields-of-grain kitchens. Our favorite kind is the large, sunny sort, with a big oak table and a roomy pantry and a garden out the back steps. The point, however, is that you can cook in most any kitchen—except for a stagnant one. (Nor should you forget that outside, all the world's a kitchen—just a little hole and some wood serves well.)

On a practical note, though, to breathe fresh life in a stagnant kitchen, make sure the oven works. Check all the burners, pilot lights, whatnot. Clean out the fridge. Clean out the cupboards. Vinegar on a rag works wonders—kills mold and freshens. Chuck old spices and flours, which go rancid and impotent after a year or so. Organize the shelves and cupboards so the most needful things are within easiest reach, and clustered according to purpose (serving dishes, baking stuff, pots and pans, dry goods). Clean up the counters and cutting surfaces and try to keep them as uncluttered as possible—infrequently used kitchen gadgets should not be allowed to take up prime kitchen real estate. Rosanna's toaster sits atop the unused dryer in the laundry room.

NOTES ON EQUIPMENT

Storage

Ken is a potter, and his kitchen is full of hand-thrown bowls and jugs. Rosanna scavenges lots of Mason jars and crocks from thrift stores for food storage, pickling, brewing, and whatnot. Be wary: Sometimes urban thrift stores will try to sell you Mason jars for more than they cost new at the hardware store. Make sure you have good, new canning lids for the jars if you want to do any canning.

Cooking and Baking Dishes

There is no substitute for a good cast-iron skillet (see "Caring for Cast Iron," below). A heavy cast-iron Dutch oven, enameled or not, is versatile for braising and stewing and even baking, too. Look for heavy stainless-steel sheet pans for drying, baking, and roasting; and glass, enamel, or stoneware pie tins if you don't have enough skillets. A baking stone will make a world of difference for your breads and pizzas. A big stockpot saves time and energy, and an assortment of smaller saucepans will round out your collection.

Knives

Keep them sharp and hone them regularly with a steel. You really only need a big chef's knife, a small paring knife, and maybe a serrated knife for bread and ripe tomatoes. But please do invest in the best knife you can afford. A great knife will cost less than $100 and it is the most important purchase you can make. A kitchen without a decent sharp knife and a good stable wooden cutting board is like a cart without a horse—it goes nowhere.

Utensils

There are only a few utensils every kitchen should have: a few stout wooden spoons (olive or bamboo work nicely), several mixing bowls of diverse sizes, a metal flipper-spatula. A rubber scraper-spatula is also handy, along with a whisk and a ladle. A candy thermometer is useful, if you really have to know. A heavy rolling pin is a must. A sturdy meat tenderizer, or an Italian *batticarne* (a neat little disk with a handle, ideal for gently pounding meat) is a lot of fun. A little salt cellar is indispensable next to the stove. And a good mortar and pestle is priceless. Seriously, we are *not* into gadgets for their own sake. And never buy anything that serves only one purpose. Waste of money and space. On the other hand, a food mill is a treasure.

Tea Towels and Cheesecloth

By "tea towel" we don't mean something made of terry cloth. You need a towel to throw over the rising dough and tie over the pickle crock, and you'd rather it not stick to the dough. Several smooth, sturdy cloths, maybe three square feet, will do the trick. You'll also want good, *fine* mesh cheesecloth for straining. A piece of old sheeting will do in a pinch.

CARING FOR CAST IRON

Teflon breaks down at high temperatures, causes cancer, and winds up flaking away in bits of tawdry chintz. Cast iron lasts for centuries, costs little, heats evenly, imparts great color and texture, doubles as a baking dish, looks gorgeous, and even leaves trace amounts of nutritious iron in your food. When cared for properly, it provides a better nonstick surface than Teflon.

1. **Quest for your iron.** Look in the darkened corners of antique stores, free boxes, other people's basements, and your grandmother's broiler drawer for brands like Griswold, Wagner, or Sidney. Lodge, which is the most widely available brand nowadays, has a coarse, grainy surface that doesn't create quite a perfectly slick nonstick surface when seasoned. Keep in mind that the best skillets may lurk under centuries of rusty grode.

2. **Refine your iron.** Tackle the cruddy skillet with coarse steel wool, a spoon, a pickaxe, a screwdriver. Alternatively, you can set cast iron in the coals of a hot campfire or fireplace for several hours and simply cook off a hundred years' dross.

3. **Polish your iron.** Seasoning is the gradual process of creating a legit nonstick surface, by saturating the iron's minutely porous surface with fats. The best thing is to ask a bear slayer for some of the leftover fat, and slowly render that fat on low heat for hours and hours. A good rubdown with other fats is sufficiently effec-

tive. Saturated animal fats or refined tropical oils are the best, as butter has milk solids that will burn, and oils go rancid quickly. Ken swears by duck fat to season pans and woks. Coat the cast iron well and set it in a warm oven for several hours or overnight. Or if you really have guts, put it in the barbecue with the lid closed and crank up the heat. A few successive coatings of fat will give you a great nonstick sheen. Just wear good oven mitts!

After cast iron has been seasoned up, its care is a matter of simple maintenance. Since the whole point of this endeavor is to build up a fat-based nonstick layer in the skillet, don't wash it with soap. Depending on its dirtiness, just wipe the skillet out, or rinse with hot water. You can scrub it vigorously and scour it with salt or abrasive sponges if you need to. That's the lovely thing about iron seasoning: It's not just an easily flaked superficial coating, but permeates the skillet like good character. Just don't soak or soap it, or heat it without oil (for example, cooking tortillas on high dry heat will burn off your pretty seasoning). Think of it like your skin. After its bath, it wants to be dried right away and greased up. Set it on a warm burner just till the water evaporates, give it a spoonful of bacon grease or coconut oil, rub it in, and hang the skillet somewhere prominent.

The skillet numbering system was no doubt developed during that era when dress sizes, wire gauges, ounces, and USB cords were all getting standardized. A No. 3 skillet is six inches in diameter; a No. 8, eleven inches.

1
Ferments of Vegetables and Legumes

Fermentation is a magical process involving the bacteria that are teeming everywhere, both outside and inside our bodies. (Think about that when you reach for some disinfectant soap.) Making fermented vegetables is basically just a matter of leaving them in salty water and letting the bacteria do their work—encouraging the good ones and discouraging the bad. In the past, this process was crucial to our survival through the winter, especially in colder climates. Today, we have the luxury of buying fresh produce year-round, shipped from the far corners of the earth at great expense, but in the past a vegetable in winter was either a stored root like a turnip, or it was fermented. The word *pickling* is used fairly loosely today, and includes vegetables that are really only brined and marinated in vinegar. This does make sense in hot climates, especially because just as the cukes and cabbage are ready to harvest, the weather will be far too hot for fermentation. This is why you find pickles in northern Germany but not in southern Italy. While these marinated vegetables can be nice, they pale beside the real thing, and you must believe that what you can make at home is infinitely superior to a supermarket jar.

Pickles

At the farmers' market one blistering day in August, I spotted perfect, fat, zeppelin-shaped cucumbers, longing to achieve apotheosis through pickling. When I muse on the idea of the Platonic Pickle, it is never sweet, tainted with turmeric, sliced into spears or rounds, diminutive like a wimpy French *cornichon*, flaccid, or in any way marred by pasteurization. The whole point of a true pickle is the bacteria that make it sour, which experts contend promote digestive health. Pasteurization kills everything, including the flavor, so for a real pickle, you should do it yourself. We are going for the real pickle, the mother of all pickles. So sour your face twists. So garlicky you stink for a week. So crunchy it sounds like biting into an apple. So kosher it makes you curse in Yiddish. This pickle is a fat and warty Leviathan. Gripped with a whole fist, it doubles as a lethal weapon.

Surprisingly, pickles are simple to make; they demand no canning or complicated equipment. People have been making pickles like these for centuries, long before pasteurization. The only problem I encountered on my first trial was heat. In the Central Valley of California, where it can hover over 100 degrees for weeks on end, letting pickles ferment on the countertop is begging for disaster. Experiment number one involved a few pounds of beautiful unwaxed zeppelin-shaped cukes in a stoneware crock, with peppercorns, coriander, dill fronds, and garlic. This was covered in brine (just tap water and enough salt to float an egg) and left to do its business for two weeks. They smelled like pickles. Looked like pickles. Yet when I pulled one from the crock it literally exploded in my hands. It was hollow and filled with noxious gas. They had become not pickles, but hand grenades. Obviously something had gone terribly wrong.

As it turns out, 80 degrees is the absolute upper limit for beneficial bacteria to thrive and dominate the brine. Any hotter and the evil beasties take over. Not even my stalwart air-conditioning could save these from infiltration. For those of you with a cellar, this is the ideal solution. My cellar, an oddity in the Central Valley, since we are 13 feet above sea level, would have worked fine, but it is filled with pottery equipment, glaze chemicals, and clay dust. It is a basement pottery studio, and when I fire the kiln, the space rises well over 100 degrees. I realize I am breaking the rule of historical authenticity here, but there is a good solution for those without a cellar. The fridge is too cold, but a wine fridge is perfect, kept at about 55 to 65 degrees. In my mind that's too cold for red wine, and not cold enough for white. So out came the bottles and in went the pickles. This became my makeshift cellar for many of the recipes that appear in this book. A root cellar dug outside the house would also work perfectly, but not everyone has the luxury of a yard to dig up.

The recipe: Start with a large glass jar or ceramic crock big enough to hold fat pickles, about four or five inches in length. Pour boiling water in the crock to sterilize it for a minute or so, then pour out the water. Don't use antibacterial dish soap, because this will kill many of the guys you want alive. Heavily chlorinated water will do the same. Rinse off the pickles and place them in the jar with enough space at the top to cover. Add the spices, which might include dill fronds or seeds, peeled garlic cloves, whole peppercorns, and coriander. Fennel seed is also a nice twist.

Pour brine over, which is best made with kosher salt; use half a cup (eight tablespoons) of salt to eight cups of water, which equals half a gallon. Add a quarter cup of vinegar, which many people do to play it safe with the level of acidity. You can double the whole recipe, if you like. Also, you can use less salt if you like milder pickles, about six tablespoons to a half gallon of water, which is about a 5 percent solution.

Place a small dish inside the mouth of the crock with a weight on top to keep the pickles submerged. Some people contend that a grape leaf helps the whole process. Cherry leaves are also supposed to work. Don't cover with a lid, but you can tie a cloth over it if you are afraid of dust in the cellar or bugs.

Let the jar sit undisturbed in a cool place for 25 days. Remove any mold from the top if any develops. From the jar should emerge the most beautifully light green, extremely sour and salty, fat and seriously pickled pickles on earth. From there, you either eat them all in the next week or so, or put them in the fridge, which stops the fermentation, where they will keep for months. But I doubt they will last that long. The fridge also mellows out the saltiness when they first emerge from the brine. These go very well sliced lengthwise on a toasted baguette with smoked turkey and a good stinky cheese, arugula, and a dab of mayo. Breakfast!

—K

HISTORIC PICKLE RECIPES

Of Cucumbers

Take a kettle big enough for your use, full of water, make it brackish with salt, boyle therein ten or twenty Cucumbers, cut in halves, then take the raw cucumbers, being somewhat little, and put them into a vessell wherein you will keep them, and when your liquor is cold straine so much of it into them, as many keep the Cucumbers alwayes covered.

To Pickle Cucumbers to Keep All the Yeare

Pare a good quantity of the rindes of cucumbers, and boyle them in a quart of running water, and a pint of wine Vinegar, with a handfull of salt, till they be soft, then letting them stand till the liquor be quite cold pour out the liquor from the rinds, into some little barrell, earthen pot, or other vessel, that may be close stopped, and put as many of the youngest Cucumbers you can gather, therein, as the liquor will cover, and so keep them close covered, that no wind come to them, to use all the year till they have new; if your Cucumbers be great, tis best to boyle them in the liquor till they be soft.

From the Anonymous *A Book of Fruits and Flowers*.
London: M.S. for Tho. Jenner, 1656.

Sauerkraut

Building on your pickling skills, proceed next to real fermented unpasteurized raw sauerkraut, which is actually simpler than any pickle. The bacteria that turn cabbage or any vegetable into a pickle are literally everywhere. It is a pity that we think of bacteria as enemies. Sure, there are some that can harm us. Our bodies usually learn to fight these off, unless we are crammed with antibiotics, which do the job for us. But most of the bacteria we live with, and of course evolved with, are beneficial for our bodies. That we can even think of ecology as preserving flora and fauna, while we obliterate bacteria without blinking an eye—in the soil, in the kitchen, on our hands, seems the most remarkable example of speciesism. We should care about bacteria, yeasts, and other microbes, mostly because they give us flavors we crave instinctually: pickles, yeasty bread, stinky cheese, not to mention alcohol. More on this anon. First here follow four variations on kraut, all of which use the same basic brine.

The classic recipe is simple. Cut white cabbage finely or grate it. I use three small organic cabbages equaling two and a half pounds, which almost fills a quart jar. One large cabbage works fine (or two, equaling about five pounds, if you want to make a gallon). Put the cut cabbage in a bowl and add two tablespoons kosher salt and knead by hand for about 10 minutes. Voilà, it makes its own luscious brine. You will not need to add any water, or anything else for that matter. Transfer the cabbage to a crock or jar, weigh it down with a plate or ceramic jar lid so everything is submerged, and pop it into the "cellar." Let it sit for three or four weeks at a cool temperature. You will end up with beautifully sour, crunchy, and piquant sauerkraut. You can also do this on the kitchen counter if you keep the temperature around 70 degrees; it will work much faster, perhaps as quick as a week, but will not be quite as complex in flavor. Be sure to taste it often, and when you like it, it's ready to eat.

Sauerkraut is lovely cooked. Romanians cook it slowly with butter and paprika for a few hours until brown. The dish is called *varsalita*, and it is always on my Thanksgiving table. A few caraway seeds thrown in won't hurt, either. One can also stew the kraut slowly with onions and apples, perhaps with a few sausages tossed in.

Red Cabbage

I've wondered why no one pickles red cabbage the way sauerkraut is fermented. All recipes for red cabbage are vinegared and sugared, but why not fermented? That sounds good—sweet and sour and crunchy. First, understand that red cabbage is its own wonderful creature—nature's own litmus paper. As a science fair project, boil red cabbage and then dye sheets of ordinary paper in the liquid. The dried paper will then test for bases and acids, turning green with a base and red with an acid. Baking soda and lime juice work best, and you can make some lovely tricolored decorative end papers with these three ingredients alone.

For red cabbage, take one large honking head, quartered, cored, and finely shredded with a knife, and mix it with three tablespoons salt and nothing else. Leave this overnight in a bowl, to draw off moisture and let the cabbage cells absorb the salt. Prepare some vinegar by boiling it with spices. I usually go a little overboard and use cloves, pepper, a few slices of nutmeg, cubebs, and cassia buds. The latter two are medieval spices, or at least that's the last time they were used in European cuisine, but black pepper and a cinnamon stick will do just fine. You can add a quarter cup of sugar in the vinegar to sweeten. Leave the mixture to cool overnight. The next day, rinse the cabbage and fill two quart-size jars (you may need to cram it down). Over this pour the spiced vinegar, weight the cabbage with a plate, and leave it to ferment in a cool cellar.

The fermenting process should take two or three weeks. The red sauerkraut you'll end up with goes lovely with a schnitzel, or pork chop. A lovely smoked chop, *Kassler knacken*, like they have in Germany, would be perfect. With potato dumplings, oh! The amazing thing about this red cabbage is its indestructibility; the color and bright flavor will not fade with time.

Pickle Variations on a Theme

I have to admit, I stole the idea of throwing anything at hand into the pickle jar. At the Berkeley farmers' market there is a beautiful organic sauerkraut lady who sells fermented shredded red beets with fennel. It is one of the most delicious things I have ever tasted. Try pickled yellow beets or a fennel bulb pickled separately, which are simple riffs on this. Simply peel and coarsely shred raw beets with a box grater and cover with brine (two tablespoons of salt and enough water to cover). This will fill a little half-liter jar, and is stunning to look at. The fennel takes the same treatment, adorned with its own fronds. Ferment them in a cool spot for a few weeks. Both are an intriguing twist on sauerkraut. After this, have fun using bok choy or other forms of cabbage, throw in garlic and chili peppers, and you will have one beautiful *kimchi*. Turnips diced also make intriguing pickles, as do carrots. Feel free to experiment and throw in whatever strikes your fancy.

—*K*

Olives

Olives are the perfect food. Even breakfast for me pales without a few big honking Cerignolas to get the day started. They are also surprisingly simple to cure—assuming you have a source for raw olives, that is. I started with dozens of olive trees growing along the streets in Stockton, which make a big mess along March Lane and Pacific Avenue, so no one minded my taking them. The traffic and exhaust fumes left me rather unsettled though. For several years thereafter I was fortunate enough to have a local winery nearby that let me pick a shopping bag full every fall. Otherwise, they fell on the ground. This lasted until recently; now they press the olives for oil. Makes sense. Nothing else to do but plant my own trees and wait the 12 years for a full harvest. Still, this year and last I got a good-size jar from them.

Here's the procedure. Pick the olives just when they are beginning to go from green to purplish. Crack the olives one by one with a hammer—gently, so they just barely split. You will get a little splattered with oil, which stains permanently, so if you are averse to such a badge of honor, cover them in a tea towel. Also, if you really bash them, after the cure they will look like monkey brains, as my friend called them. Soak the slightly cracked olives in water, changing the water daily and taking a nibble daily until all the bitterness is gone. This can take one or two weeks, depending on the size. Then put them in brine (water and enough salt to float an egg, plus any seasonings you like). Bay leaves are great, as are other herbs. After a couple of weeks, they should taste nice and salty and pungent. Store in the fridge, or can them in sterile Mason jars.

You can also slow-cure them, which takes about eight months to a year. The procedure here is even simpler. Just throw the olives into the brine with seasonings and forget about them in a cool, dark corner. No cracking, no preliminary soaking is necessary. They will get moldy on top, but never you mind. It creates a kind of plug. The bitterness will slowly seep out, and the flavor will become much more complex than the quick cure. If after this time they still taste a little bitter, just change the brine. The last batch I made took a full 14 months, with about three changes of brine in the final three months. They were the best I've ever made, and sit happily on the counter in a big glass jar.

—K

Lupins

Lupins, although a bean, are similar to olives aesthetically, and are equally good with breakfast. The trick is first to soak them overnight until rehydrated, then boil them for a few hours like any bean. They will not soften. Then soak them again, changing the water every day for several weeks until the bitterness is gone. It's a very long, slow, and tedious process. I have heard of people leaving them in the tub under the running faucet, which I guess replicates a running stream. After that they are brined just like olives, again with whatever herbs you like. They never get soft, and remain slightly crunchy. You can peel off the outer skin of each bean with your teeth if you like, but remember, they are always eaten cold as a snack. There is no way to cook them to softness like other beans. Store these in a jar covered in brine in the fridge; they will keep indefinitely.

—*K*

Koji Mold

What could be witchier than cultivating a powerful mold right in your kitchen? You send away for some magic spores, and when they arrive in a tiny nondescript envelope, you scramble about getting things in readiness, fussing over proper incubation temperatures, muttering to yourself as you fluff a rice bed and bundle the swaddling towels. At last, you sprinkle a green powder over some rice and wait with bated breath for the mold to accept your ministrations and multiply. Hours later, it stirs in its bedding, sending up a sweet, fecund aroma and radiating its own pulsing, living heat. Honestly, molds make magnificent pets . . . or minions. Allies? Lesser divinities?

The mold I'm talking about is quite different from your standard rank, rotting, spoilage molds, and even quite different from the blossoming cheese-molds on brie and Roquefort and the like. It is a grain mold, *Aspergillus oryzae*, which the Chinese and Japanese have been cultivating for millennia. It's usually grown on steamed rice, where it gives the rice a fluffy white coating. As the mold colonizes a rice grain, it produces powerful enzymes that make it extremely useful for fermenting other foods, like miso, vegetables, or (in the case of sake) more rice.

You can find ready-made *koji* in a well-stocked Japanese grocery store, brewing supply store, or natural food store; or you can order it from the Internet. It should be as fresh as possible—no more than a month old, ideally. You can also make it yourself, if you mail-order some spores.

In fact, culturing *koji* really only takes a weekend's worth of attention, after which you can set aside your symbiotic responsibilities and resume your social life.

I've adapted the directions to suit the average kitchen. First, of course, you'll need some spores. You can order them online (see Resources), or inquire with a local miso or sake maker. After that, the trickiest part is (1) setting aside the time and (2) assembling an incubator, and even that's not very difficult (see "The Incubator," page 15). Beyond that, you'll just need to have ready a clean bath towel (if you haven't got a lovely wooden sushi box), a two-foot-square finely woven cloth (like a piece of an old bed sheet), a thermometer that can give you measurements between 80 and 120 degrees, a square yard of loose-weave cloth (like cheesecloth), and a steamer. If you don't have a dumpling steamer basket, one of those expandable vegetable steamer inserts and a large pot will do the trick just fine, though you will have to elevate the steamer to keep the rice several inches off the bottom of the pot (a tin can with both ends removed will work).

Here's how it works.

PREPARING THE RICE

Rice for *koji* wants to be as nonsticky and mushy as possible. Regular boiled rice will fall apart when cultured; instead, steam it. First, in the morning when you want to make *koji*, rinse six cups of polished rice repeatedly to remove all the powdery starch on the outside. Rinse till the water runs clear. Add twice as much water as rice and let soak for an hour.

Drain the rice in a colander for several minutes, then spread it out on a kitchen towel to dry for 15 minutes. Place the rice in your steamer (see above) and pour a couple of inches of water in the bottom of the pot. Line the steamer bed with enough cheesecloth to hang over the edges of the pot and dump in the rice. (You want the cheesecloth to be large, as you'll be using it to lift the rice out of the pot when it's done.) Spread the rice

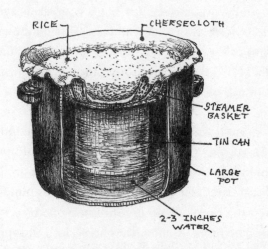

To steam rice for koji, *put two to three inches of water in the bottom of a large pot. Prop a steamer basket above the water on a tin can, and line the basket with fine cheesecloth.*

into an even layer, right up to the edge of the pot, so no steam gets a chance to escape. Fold the overhanging cheesecloth back over the rice. Cover the pot or basket with its lid and bring to a boil. After it's reached a full, rolling boil, steam the rice for 50 minutes. When the rice is done, it should look transparent but not be at all cohesive like ordinary cooked rice.

PREPARING THE MOLD

While the rice steams, make its bed and ready the spores. In a dry skillet, lightly toast a quarter cup of flour to sanitize it. Pour it into a small bowl, and when it's cool, add a teaspoon of spores. Do check the packaging, as some producers may pre-dilute the spores—in which case, they will tell you how much spore-powder to add. Mix the spores into the flour well—this will help you distribute them evenly throughout the rice.

On your work surface, lay out a couple of layers of thick terry-cloth towels covering at least a two-foot-wide square. The point of the towels is to keep your *koji* contained in something that's breathable, moisture-trapping, and insulating all at once. On top of the towels, place your square of clean cotton sheeting. A clean wooden box of the right size can replace the towels, though you would still want to line the interior with a sheet. Have your thermometer ready. You could probably get by without it for now, but you'll want to check on the temperature of your rice later on, without opening its bundle.

When the rice is done, use the cheesecloth to transfer it to the cotton bedding. Remove the cheesecloth and spread out the rice to a depth of about one inch, and stick the thermometer in it. Stir once or twice until it's evenly cooled to 113 degrees; the rice should feel lightly warm to the touch.

THE INCUBATOR

You want to create the perfect environment to foster mold growth, which means a steady, warm temperature and plenty of humidity. A picnic cooler lined with towels and hot water bottles works well, as does sticking a 60-watt lightbulb in the bottom of your oven. Whatever method you use, you will have to monitor the temperature and adjust it regularly, as partway through the culturing process, the mold itself begins to give off heat. If the mold gets too hot, it can kill itself. Aim for a steady 85 degrees, opening the oven door or changing the hot water bottles as necessary. To increase humidity, place a small dish of water near your heat source, and periodically sprinkle the sheeting around your *koji* with cool, clean water.

Sprinkle half of the flour-spore mixture over the rice. Stir, then spread it out again and sprinkle it with the rest of the flour-spore mixture. Stir thoroughly, then gather up the corners and edges of the sheet to pull the rice into a tight bundle. Stick the thermometer in the middle, poking out the top, and wrap the towel layers around the sheet. Your ideal temperature is about 85 degrees. Tuck your bundle into its prepared incubator and let it go to work. You'll want to check back on it throughout the day.

WATCHING THE *KOJI*

This is the hard part! Keep checking the temperature every few hours, making any necessary adjustments (refilling water bottles, moving lightbulbs, etc.) to keep the *koji* at 85 degrees. Slight temperature variation is unavoidable, but don't let it go below 77 or above 95 degrees.

After 24 hours, the *koji* will be making its own magic heat. Not only will the thermometer start climbing, but you'll be able to feel heat coming off the *koji* itself. (In fact, *koji* makers of old used to heat their *koji* cellars with nothing but the warmth of fermenting *koji*!) At this point you must change your tactics. You'll need to help the *koji* stay evenly warm and humid without cooking itself.

Unwrap the bundle (it should smell like sweet cheese and chestnuts!) and spread the rice out into two large, deep, clean pans. Draw one-inch furrows in the rice two inches apart to allow heat to escape, cover with the sheeting and towels (not so tightly this time), and return it to the incubator. You probably won't need the lightbulb or hot water bottles anymore unless your house is quite cold. Monitor the temperature closely— don't let the mixture get above 104 degrees at this point. If the rice clumps too much, it will get hot enough to kill the mold. You also need to keep the rice humid. If you keep the rice in a cooler, you can put a pan of warm water inside the cooler and set the *koji* pans on top. Or put a pan of warm water in the oven.

Let the rice continue to grow for another 24 hours. During this time, it will develop a fluffy white coat, and form webby clumps between grains. Yes, you may have to get up in the middle of the night to check the temperature and stir it around. It's worth it.

To check the rice for doneness, break a grain in half. It should break easily, and the layer of white mold on the outside should penetrate two-thirds of the way into the grain.

Spread out the finished *koji* on several large baking sheets to cool down and dry. Pour it into glass jars, lid it tightly, and store it in the refrigerator. It loses potency after about a month.

TO SAVE YOUR OWN SPORES

After making a batch of *koji*, you can sprinkle half a cup of *koji* on a plate, cover it loosely, and put it back in the incubator. The mold will continue to develop, and after another two days, will develop a greenish-yellow spore coating. Let the rice dry out thoroughly, grind it, and store it for your next batch of *koji*.

Koji Pickles

Shred one small head of cabbage. Mix it with two tablespoons salt and knead it with your hands to help extract the juice. Put it in a large jar or crock with a weight inside, pressing down on the cabbage. Let it sit for a day in the refrigerator. The next day, stir in a large handful of *koji* rice and leave the jar to ferment in a cupboard for a day or two, then refrigerate. The cabbage will keep for months in the refrigerator; eventually getting too mushy to eat plain. These pickles are fantastic—they taste tangy, mild, and slightly sweet. You can pickle most any vegetable with *koji*; certain types may not have the longevity of cabbage. Proceed similarly, chopping the vegetables and brining them overnight before mixing in the *koji*.

Miso

Fermenting your own miso is delightful and shockingly easy. Just cook and mash soybeans, add salt and *koji*, and put it away in a cupboard. *Koji* mold produces powerful enzymes that break down the proteins and carbohydrates in soybeans, turning them into potent flavor compounds.

SWEET WHITE MISO

The more *koji* you use, the lighter and sweeter your miso will be, and the quicker it will ferment. This recipe has a high proportion of *koji* and makes a sweet-salty miso.

Soak two cups of dry soybeans overnight in plenty of water. The next morning, pour off the soaking water, add plenty of fresh water, and cook the beans until so soft you can easily crush one between the thumb and ring finger of your nondominant hand. Soybeans take at least half a day to cook.

When they're quite done, drain the beans, saving the cooking liquid. Let them both cool to a comfortable temperature and mash the beans with a potato masher. You can leave some of the beans whole or chunky for a textured miso, or mash them smooth if you prefer. Measure a cup of cooled cooking liquid and stir in one-quarter cup of sea salt until dissolved. Stir this into the mashed beans along with four cups of *koji* rice. You can add more bean cooking liquid to achieve a spreadable paste.

Pack the miso in a clean crock, pushing out any air pockets, smooth the top, and sprinkle a tablespoon of salt over it. Cover the miso surface with a clean plate or lid that fits as tightly as possible inside the crock, and fill a quart jar with water. Set the jar on top of the lid as a weight to keep the miso submerged under the brine that will form. Secure a tea towel over the whole thing to keep critters out and set it in a warm, quiet spot in your kitchen (like a high cupboard).

After a month, sample the miso. It should be delicious, without a hint of alcohol or mustiness. You can use it now, or let it ferment for a few weeks longer—but do be warned that sweet miso will turn alcoholic if left too long, especially in warm weather. Since white miso ferments for such a short time, the *koji* grains will retain some crunch in the finished product. You can put the miso through a meat grinder to make it smooth, or just mash it with a fork each time you use it.

This recipe scales well if you want to make larger quantities.

Put a plate on the surface of the miso inside the crock. A jar of water on top weights the miso as it ferments.

RED MISO

Red miso requires a bit more commitment than white miso. Not only does it take a year or more to ferment, but it also produces the best results when made in a relatively large quantity. Small quantities of miso have a high ratio of surface area to volume, and miso is most vulnerable on its surfaces.

Red miso is traditionally made when the weather is cool, so that its own microorganisms can get a foothold before the heat of summer encourages alcohol-producing yeasts. You can make red miso just like white miso, with the following changes.

Use four cups of dry soybeans and half a cup of salt. When you mix the salt with the cooking liquid, be *quite* sure that the water's comfortable to the touch, and mix in a tablespoon of good-quality *unpasteurized* red miso, which you can find in a well-stocked grocery store. Adding this "seed" miso gives some special microorganisms a jump-start. Mix in the same quantity of *koji* (four cups) as for white miso.

When you go to pack the crock, first rub sea salt on the bottom and sides. A little water will help it stick. Be generous when you salt the top, too. Salt protects the miso from invasion by unfriendly bacteria.

An easy way to scale up your miso production is simply to make multiple batches over the next few days. You can pack the new miso right on top of yesterday's batch; if you do so, you only need to salt the top of the *final* batch of miso packed in the crock.

Since red miso takes so long to age, you'd do well to label the crock with the date you made it, the type of miso, and its projected finish date. Then store it in a cool place—a dry basement or attic (not during the summer!) or shed. The first time I made red miso, I followed some bad advice and put it somewhere quite warm. It turned alcoholic, and not pleasantly so. It's fine for red miso to warm up after it's had a chance to establish itself. If you live in a place without four seasons, you can emulate the rhythm of summer and winter by moving the crock from the cool place to a warmer cupboard.

After a year (including at least one warm season), unpack the miso. Don't worry if there's some superficial mold; just scrape it off and try the miso underneath. Savory, meaty, complicated? Take some out for immediate use and refrigerate it. Smooth and salt the top of the remaining miso, and let it keep fermenting.

MISO SOUP

You can do a hundred amazing things with miso, but the best will always be a simple miso soup. Here's the gist: Make a flavorful broth of some sort (or don't, as plain water is fine, too), and add a little bit of miso at the very end when the heat is off. If the miso is cooked, it dies. In traditional Japanese cooking, the broth is called *dashi*, or soup stock. Unlike Western soup stocks, *dashi* takes little time to prepare.

Bring to a boil as much water as you want for your soup. As it heats, add a piece of kombu seaweed and a sprinkling of dried bonito flakes to taste. When it boils, turn off the heat and let it sit for 10 minutes. Strain it (or don't) and add the miso paste—about a tablespoon per cup of liquid, or however strong you like it. Sprinkle with minced green onion.

Variations: Try a little grated ginger, minced garlic, wakame seaweed, daikon, tofu, or carrots. You can crack in an egg after the soup is done and the heat has been turned off. Let it sit long enough for the whites to cook.

—*R*

2

Fresh Vegetables and Legumes

In the midst of summer's bounty, cooking is nearly effortless and sometimes purely optional. The hard part, traditionally, has been finding ways to preserve summer's bounty for the coming winter. (Nowadays, the hard part is finding enough fuel to truck our vegetables and fruits across hemispheres so we can eat stale, graying produce all the year through.) Still, for those not used to living by gardens, summer's bounty can be rather overwhelming. What do you do when faced with a bushel of ripe tomatoes from the garden or on sale in August at the farmers' market? How are you supposed to deal with three heads of lettuce a day for the next 10 weeks? This is the reason traditional recipes don't call for half a tomato, and why you should make every effort to get ripe tomatoes when they are abundant. Quite simply, it's a snap to cook with local produce, because fresh, ripe produce is delicious to begin with.

The bounty doesn't even end in September. Lots of delicious produce survives the winter very well with minimal care—root crops, nuts, dry beans, hard winter squash, apples, and cabbages, for example. And leafy greens, like escarole and chard and kale, will grow long past the first frost (or even the whole winter through).

The recipes in this chapter represent a few of our favorite ways for cooking with fresh and bountiful vegetables.

Fresh Tomato Sauce

This sauce probably defies everything you have ever read about a good tomato sauce. It does not take hours simmering on the stovetop. It is simplicity itself, and actually tastes mostly of tomatoes. The tomatoes have to be good, but the variety really doesn't matter. I'd rather use a good vine-ripened beefsteak than a pithy, flavorless Roma. Talk to the tomatoes gently, and reassure them that the ordeal they are about to undergo will be worth it, though quick and violent. First heat a capacious skillet on the highest flame. Cut the tomatoes (maybe a dozen) in half only. No need to do anything else. Smash a clove of garlic, but leave it in its skin. Roughly peel and chop an onion. Pull the leaves from a few sprigs of fresh oregano; maybe rosemary, too, if you like. Then add a good quantity of oil to the pan—perhaps half a cup, if you have guts. It will begin to smoke immediately. Throw in the tomatoes. Do nothing. Let them sear, char, incinerate. Actually, what you're trying to do is get some decent caramelization without the tomatoes oozing water and boiling. Add in the remaining ingredients, but don't stir. Throw in some salt and a few grinds of pepper. You should be building up some good gunk on the bottom of the pan. Call it "fond," if you like. After about five minutes, glug some red wine in the pan and stir it up. Let mixture cook another five minutes.

Turn the food mill to pass cooked tomato pulp through, leaving behind seeds and skin.

Next, find a food mill. It is a simple contraption that removes seeds and skins—invaluable in a traditional kitchen. Or barring that, use a fine-mesh strainer or "China hat." Pass the sauce through the mill into a bowl, leaving behind the skins and seeds. Then return the sauce to the pan. Drop your pasta in the water. Boil until still toothsome. Remove from the water, drain in a colander if you like (but do not rinse or you will wash away all the good starch that helps the sauce stick!), and place directly into the pan with the sauce. Or if you prefer the sauce served on top, feel free. There should be a lot more pasta than sauce. Give it a taste for salt. Serve with a wedge of Parmigiano-Reggiano (only the real stuff) for grating.

Easy Tomato Sauce

There is another way to make fresh quick tomato sauce, a little easier and with a more delicate flavor. For this one, place a regular saucepan on medium heat. Add olive oil and begin to cook some chopped onions and garlic. Place over the pan a flat, large-holed grater. Cut the tomatoes in half and grate them, cut side down, directly into the pot. At the end you will have just the skin. The seeds do go in this sauce, but it is none the worse for it. This should be cooked only for a few minutes, but you can also leave it on the stove for a long time for a deeper, richer sauce if you think it is too watery, or better yet, cook some vegetables in it, like green Romano beans. In this case add a good pour of olive oil, a cup of water, and some basil leaves, and slowly simmer for an hour or longer. It is divine.

—*K*

Beans and Greens Soup

Take a cup of dried beans and soak them overnight. You want a firm bean that will keep its shape, like cannellini, though any bean will work. The next morning, drain and boil the beans gently, barely covered in plain water (without salt), until just tender. This may take anywhere from half an hour to an hour, depending on the age of the beans. There is no good way to tell the age of beans, so be sure to keep tasting for tenderness. Add these to a quart of your best chicken stock (see page 138) along with finely chopped onions, diced carrots, celery, and finely shredded greens. These can be chard, collards, Italian *cavolo nero*, or other cabbage. Simmer gently, add salt to taste plus herbs such as fresh oregano or crushed fennel. Let mixture simmer for perhaps an additional half hour so the flavors all come together. Serve with a dash of olive oil and a grating of fresh Parmigiano-Reggiano. If you have leftovers, throw in some stale bread grated directly into the pot and you'll have an approximation of what is called *ribbolita* in Tuscany, meaning reboiled.

—*K*

Onion Soup

I absolutely adore traditional French onion soup, and I am very fussy about how it's made, because there are so many poor versions. It is really easy to do well; it just takes time. I will leave you the option here of using plain water or chicken stock. They are both very tasty. I hesitate to recommend beef stock, because to my mind it overwhelms the onion flavor. It still tastes good, especially with ground allspice or five-spice powder, but perhaps a little too intense.

The key is to bisect the onion (a plain yellow onion works best), and remove the top and bottom and skins. Then, with the cut side facing down, slice the onion into the thinnest possible semicircles. The shreds will of course naturally come apart along each layer. Cook these shreds gently in a pan with butter and a few pinches of salt and dried thyme. I use an onion per person with a pat of butter per person. If you want a big, meal-size serving for two, double that. Cook the onions on a low flame as long as you possibly can, stirring frequently, until they are dark and caramelized and smell sweet. This should take maybe an hour. There's nothing worse than flaccid, undercooked onions. The longer you spend on this step, the better the final product.

Next add your water or chicken stock to cover by a few inches. If you want thick soup, add less. Cook an additional half hour or so, and then taste for salt. Ladle the soup into separate oven-proof bowls with narrow tops. Place on top of each bowl a raft of buttered toast slices, made from the best baguette you can find. The onions will hold it aloft. On top of that add a good handful of coarsely grated Gruyère. You can be imaginative with the cheese. Anything you can grate will work, but the strings created by Gruyère, Emmenthaler, and the like are half the fun. Bake at 350 degrees until the cheese is melted and bubbly and dripping over the sides of the bowl. Serve with a ruddy French red wine, and be sure to pour some into the bowl when you're done, for swigging out the last bit of onion.

—K

Gazpacho

For years I made gazpacho the lazy way: a can of tomato juice or V8, some canned chicken stock, Tabasco and Worcestershire sauces, and some chopped vegetables in the soup and on the side for garnish. Chill and serve. It tastes okay, almost like a Bloody Mary really, so you might as well slosh some vodka in this swill. Then I tasted real gazpacho in Spain, and even better is its thicker sibling, a *salmorejo cordobés*, which I tasted in Córdoba. I have never again looked at a can. This recipe is truly incredible. All you need is a big mortar. (I won't say anything about a blender, if you happen to be in a rush.) Think of this soup as cold liquid salad. It must never see anything of animal origin. (Except maybe a slice of ham or hardboiled egg on top.)

Start with the ripest, loveliest tomatoes you can find. This is only a soup for summer. Chop them coarsely and throw them into your mortar. If you are averse to skins, pass them through a food mill or grate them into the mortar, leaving the skins behind. Add some stale bread, and let it become soft in the tomato liquid for a few minutes. Then add any other vegetables you like that can be pounded: cucumber or peppers, a clove of garlic, but no carrots at this point because they are impossible to smash, though you can add them chopped later. Beat them until completely obliterated into a smooth creamy mass, all the while drizzling in the fruitiest-flavored aromatic olive oil you can find, some sea salt, and pepper. Give a dash of good sherry vinegar, too, and if you like, some smoked paprika (*Pimentón de la Vera*). This is now a *salmorejo*. Sprinkle with a hint of finely chopped vegetables and parsley. Put a slice of serrano ham on top for garnish. I contend that this is best at room temperature. Chilling too much dulls the fresh tomato flavor. If you add some cold water, it's a gazpacho. Then you can serve with some finely chopped vegetables, which people can add as they like, for a garnish.

White Gazpacho

Keeping all of the above principles in mind, think about what the Spanish did before there were tomatoes, when the cuisine was more closely linked to Moorish cookery. Start with pine nuts, at least a cup. Pound them with cold water, a clove of garlic, and salt until absolutely smooth and milky white. Adding a touch of sourness with lemon or verjuice is even better. Garnish with chopped apples and white raisins. It is as intriguing as it is refreshing.

—*K*

Fried Baby Artichokes

Any recipe with the confluence of *fried* and *baby* in the title must be good. Seriously, this is among the most exquisite comestibles imaginable. Begin by heating a pot of vegetable oil, filled no more than halfway. You can actually use olive oil for this, no matter what anyone says about the smoking point. Of course, using expensive extra virgin olive oil would be the height of profligacy. The bigger the pot, the more you can cook at once. I use a five-quart stockpot and a whole big 48-ounce bottle of oil. Heat the oil at medium heat for at least 10 or 15 minutes. You'll test it later with a dab of batter. (Or if you must, about 350 to 360 degrees should do the trick.)

Take your artichokes, which must be fresh, verdant, and firm. The smaller the better. Refuse limp, spotted, or in any way tired specimens. Working quickly, remove the outer leaves from the artichokes. Peel the stem, but leave it intact, cutting off only the brown bit at the bottom. Next cut the artichoke in half, scoop out the fuzzy bit at the center with a spoon, snip off the pointy top with a scissor and throw it into a bowl of beer, acidulated with the juice of half a lemon. A hoppy beer is a must, the bitterness of the hops complimenting the artichoke perfectly. (I recommend Sierra Nevada from California.) Speed

is of the essence here, if you want to retain the bright green color before the artichoke oxidizes. Repeat with remaining artichokes.

Next, take some all-purpose flour and add to the artichokes and beer until a nice thick batter is formed. You may have to add more beer, or adjust at your discretion. The consistency should be thicker than pancake batter, but still pourable. Season with ground marjoram, salt, and pepper. Mix thoroughly with your hands—which is the fun part. Take a dab of batter and drop it into the hot oil. If it sits there doing nothing, the oil is too cold. If it bubbles violently and browns, it is way too hot. You want a nice bubbling with the batter bobbing around enthusiastically. Place the artichokes in the pot gently by hand, without crowding, or they will stick together. After about 10 minutes, when golden brown, remove with a slotted spoon or Chinese "spider" (the copper wire thing on the end of a bamboo handle) and let drain on paper towels. Continue until all the artichokes are done. These can be eaten hot or are perfectly wonderful and still crisp at room temperature. Add a little salt if need be, but please resist the temptation to adulterate these with any kind of sauce. This would be a heinous intrusion upon the pure, unfettered taste of artichoke, beer, and fat.

In homage to my adopted city, Stockton, asparagus capital of the universe, I will concede that the above recipe works wonderfully with fat asparagus spears, trimmed at the bottom and the lower half peeled—never snapped off, which is a horrid waste. These, in the same batter as above, and after cooked, sprinkled with real grated Parmigiano-Reggiano, are, I contend, superior to those that can be bought at Stockton's Asparagus Festival, which are pretty amazing. Any vegetable works, really. Try eggplant cut into french-fry shapes, battered, fried, and, when done, sprinkled with powdered sugar. I hear you wince, but trust me.

If you must, use the above batter with a light, but assertive beer, on fish. Pollack, haddock, or cod are very pleasant. Use a firm whitefish thick enough so it won't fly apart in the fryer. Fish must, of course, be served with chips, and a pint of the same beer that went into the batter—say, an Old Speckled Hen or other good British bitter.

—*K*

Broccoli Rabe or Rapini

The perfect food in my personal pantheon, immediately below the olive, is broccoli rabe. Despite the name, it is not related to broccoli, but to rape in the turnip family, hence the utterly irresistible bitter edge. And because it is so perfect, I implore you to treat the vegetable with such respect that you do practically nothing to it but chop into bite-size pieces and sauté gently in good olive oil with a little salt until limp but still with a little bright greenness. Do not—*under any circumstances*—let me catch you plunging rabe into boiling water.

Here, also, is a more complex recipe. This is a reasonable facsimile of what my grandmother called a *pastel*, which means pie in Ladino, the medieval form of Spanish spoken by Sephardic Jews. It is usually made with phyllo, but matzo is much simpler, and is traditional during Passover. It can also be made with ground meat, but I like it best with vegetables only. Take three leeks and one onion sauteed in olive oil with salt, pepper, and a little dill. Cool this mixture and add two standard seven-ounce (200-gram) packages of feta, and six beaten eggs.

Add to that two bunches of finely chopped broccoli rabe. Collards work very nicely, too. Line a baking pan with half a box of egg matzo and sprinkle with white wine. Put the mixture on top, then another layer of matzo evenly arranged, covering the mixture completely, and soak it well with wine. Cover with foil and bake for about an hour at 350 degrees. If you use a regular pie crust and substitute ricotta salata for the feta, it will be very closely related to the Italian *torta pasqualina*, which is served on Easter. Rabe is also stupendous in a regular quiche, in which case use Gruyère or the like, and add cream. *Gevalt.*

—*K*

Yapraki or *Dolmas* (Stuffed Grape Leaves)

Roll up the rice mixture in grape leaves. First fold over the lower-left corner, then the opposite corner.

These make an incomparable appetizer, or *meze*, washed down with *raki*—the Turkish equivalent of Greek ouzo, a fiery anise-flavored alcohol. Rolling *dolmas* is painstaking but worth every minute. I never tasted a purchased version that even comes close.

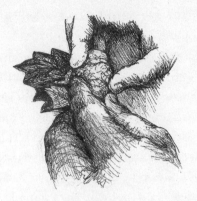

Roll the package one turn away from you. Then fold over the upper-left corner, then the right, and roll away again.

Put two cups raw rice in a bowl, add a finely chopped onion, a good deal of dill, about a quarter cup of olive oil, and the juice of a lemon. Take grape leaves, either pickled or fresh off the vine, and place them stem side toward you with the dull side up. Think of the grape leaf as a five-pointed compass with the first point on the lower left, moving clockwise around the leaf. Start with a half teaspoon or so of rice mixture, or more if the leaves are big, in the center of the leaf. Fold over the first lower-left-hand corner of the leaf. Then fold over the opposite corner. Roll the package one turn away from you. Then fold over the upper-left-hand corner, and likewise the right, and roll

Fold the uppermost section into a point and roll the whole package up so it resembles a short, blunt cigar.

away again. Fold the uppermost section into a point and roll the whole package up so it is like a short, blunt cigar.

Line a pot with a couple of grape leaves and put the first rolled *yapraki* in pointing upward, that is, not on its side. I find while filling the pot, a bunched-up cloth under the opposite end of the pot, tilting it toward you, keeps the rolls from falling over. Continue with all the other leaves until the pot is full, then move the pot to the stove. One standard jar of leaves will fill a medium saucepan. Add chicken broth or water with salt so the rolls are covered by at least half an inch. Then put a leaf or two on top to cover the rolls. Cover the pot, bring to a full boil, and then lower the heat to a gentle simmer and cook for one hour. Let cool, covered, for another hour and then serve at room temperature. You can also make these with ground lamb in the filling. Don't douse them with oil; they will be splendidly unctuous on their own. And irresistible.

—*K*

Salads and Their Dressings

Salads are ubiquitous, but alas, they're often poorly made. For starters, bottled salad dressing is one of the worst wastes of your money ever invented. It's largely composed of water, cheap oils, and emulsifiers. Get some good olive oil, a variety of vinegars, and a few herbs, and you'll be much better off financially and gustatorily.

Do also experiment with your salad greens. A good head of green-leaf lettuce is perfectly suitable, but sweet little gems are delightful, too. Members of the chicory family make delicious, colorful, crunchy salads and can often be found in the colder months—try escarole and radicchio, treviso, or endives (both curly and straight). For spice, arugula and watercress and nasturtium leaves will give you a peppery salad, and tender young dandelion greens make for a gorgeously bitter plate. Mostly, you want your greens to be washed and dried well.

And you know exactly what you like to put on your salad, no doubt. Figs, persimmons, hard-boiled eggs, goat cheese, nuts, Romano, avocado, mandarins—it's a matter of mood and character, and not something I should be telling you. The point is to make something you like.

THE BASIC VINAIGRETTE

Take a pint-size jar and pour in several tablespoons of your vinegar of choice—wine, balsamic, apple cider, champagne, rice. Add salt and pepper. While whisking with a fork, slowly dribble in three parts olive oil to your vinegar. Or lid the jar and shake it. Taste it and adjust the seasonings.

Variations:

♦ A teaspoon each of mustard and honey is nice.

♦ Some minced shallots or garlic left to macerate in the vinegar for several minutes are delightful.

♦ Use lots of honey and mustard, no vinegar, and just a little oil.

♦ Add several tablespoons maple syrup to a red wine vinaigrette.

- Add a tablespoon of curry powder to the vinegar and let sit for several minutes before adding the oil.

- Use walnut, hazelnut, or sesame oils.

- Use hot bacon drippings for the fat. Pour immediately over the salad greens to wilt them slightly.

- Use crème fraîche instead of oil, and add lots of minced dill, chives, and garlic.

- An egg yolk whisked in with the vinegar before you add any oil will make a nice creamy dressing that doesn't separate.

Most of these dressings will keep indefinitely in the refrigerator, and for a week on the pantry shelf. Anything with raw egg is less stable, of course. Dressing made with bacon drippings or olive oil may solidify in the fridge; let it come to room temperature before serving (you can warm it by setting the jar in a skillet of hot water on the stove).

MAYONNAISE

You can call it aioli. You can call it emulsified egg sauce. It's mayonnaise to me, and pure fun. When you make your own mayonnaise, you can choose what oils to put in. And let me tell you, a sparkly olive or sesame or nut oil mayonnaise is *leagues* beyond store-bought canola oil mayonnaise. Of course, a strident, grassy olive oil will make a strident, grassy mayonnaise— which may offend the palates of sensitive individuals. If, for example, you're making mayonnaise for picky kids, use a mellow olive oil blended with refined coconut oil.

Making an emulsified sauce like mayonnaise looks a little bit like kitchen wizardry. You put a liquid in another liquid, and lo and behold, you get something custardy!

Start with a good pasture-laid egg. If you're going to eat raw egg yolk, you'd better be sure it came from a happy, healthy chicken. Separate the white and use it for something else. Put the yolk in a small bowl and beat it with a fork. Add a drop of your chosen oil. Beat it. Add another drop of oil, and beat again until it's completely incorporated. Continue adding oil, drop by drop, until the mixture gains substance and gloss. As it thickens, you can add the oil in larger quantities. But do take care: too much oil and the emulsion will break. (See below when that happens.) When the mayonnaise is as thick as you like (or slightly thicker), squeeze in some lemon juice to taste and season with salt and a dab of mustard. Serve immediately or put it in a jar and store in the refrigerator for a day or two.

When the emulsion breaks: Separate another egg and put its yolk in another bowl. Drop by drop, add the broken mayonnaise, incorporating each drop thoroughly into the new egg yolk. Proceed as before.

You can make any kind of flavored mayonnaise you like. Keep in mind that the mayonnaise absorbs some flavors slowly, and you'll do well to let a flavored mayonnaise macerate in the fridge for an hour before serving it. Try any of these: a tablespoon of curry powder, ground chilis, minced garlic, or miso and soy sauce.

—R

3
Fruits and Nuts

Much romanticized for its sweet shapely abundance, good fresh fruit straight from the tree is a precious delight, and not one to be tampered with—until you have 10 bushels of peaches and no way to eat them all before they rot away. Most old-fashioned storage methods either harnessed the natural powers of fermentation and turned fruit into alcohol, or preserved it in honey; sugar, like salt, kills the microbes that cause decay. When Europe started importing cane sugar several hundred years ago, it replaced honey as the preserving tool of choice.

Nuts, fortunately, do not rot away as quickly as fruit—or, more precisely, they are often what's left *after* the fruit has rotted away. Nonetheless, our creative ancestors prepared them in many more varied ways than we tend to nowadays.

Preserves

One August back home, our landlady invited me over to finish off her blackberry bush. I got all bundled up in denim and boots and jumped in. The berries were fat and luscious in the shadowy, thorny bush—and so ripe that they collapsed under their own weight in the bucket. When I'd picked the bush clean, I had a couple of gallons of berries—but I also had only a matter of hours before I had a bucket of blackberry wine on my hands, so I rummaged about in some books, consulted Mama, and came up with a plan for making jam.

The best jam berries, I found out, are slightly underripe. Fruit won't firm up nicely without plenty of pectin, and as fruit ripens, it loses its pectin. So I went out to an apple tree and picked a hard green apple—green apples being blessed with oodles of pectin. I was so proud of my cleverness—see how I was outwitting the overripe blackberries! I minced my apple finely and added it to the berries, which I brought to a rolling boil in a large, sturdy kettle. I added some sugar and watched and stirred as a lustrous purple foam floated to the top and the boiling liquid turned sparkling black. The black bubbles got bigger and stickier and shinier, the foam denser, and the juice, yes, it even started to thicken. Success! I stirred in delight as the juice turned syrupy. Unfortunately, the hardest part of jamming is knowing when to stop. To play it safe, I boiled and boiled my blackberries, and boiled them down some more, until they really did look convincingly thick and jammy. Then I ladled the hot jam into sterilized half-pint jars, screwed down the bands, and set them on the counter where I could hear each musical "pop" as the seals formed.

The next morning, I opened a test jar and went to spread a bit of jam on my toast. My toast broke. I had a jar of blackberry leather. There are still jars and jars of that stuff in the root cellar, but you'd have to melt it a bit first to make it useful.

Heed this lesson! The jam is done *long before* it looks like jam! That said, jam is not so difficult to make. Almost any species of fruit will make a flavorful, satisfying jam—provided your specimens are remarkably delicious.

ON SELECTING FRUIT FOR PRESERVES

It's a sad truth that modern supermarket fruit is little more than colored packing foam. Your average apple has been taught since birth to be loud, shiny, and indestructible—flavor was left out of its education entirely. Though it may catch your attention all the way from the cereal aisle, it's probably stale, mealy, and covered in a stiff wax. You're much more likely to find modest fruits of spectacular flavor at a farmers' market.

The old varieties of most fruits weren't bred for storage, so don't buy them much in advance of when you need them. For small fruit, always taste before you buy. A good grocer should cut you samples of larger fruit, too, especially if you hint that you're looking to buy a jam-making quantity. And please, do us all a favor—if you taste some unremarkable fruit, tell the seller!

It's highly unlikely that you'll find any imported fruit matching your jam-making criteria. There is no substitute for fresh, local fruit in season.

Your strawberries should be dainty, completely scarlet, and (if you like them very sweet) perhaps even starting to lose their shine.

Peaches should have a deep golden glow beneath the superficial red sun-freckles. They should be dizzyingly fragrant, and their cheeks should be plump—the seam should not be at all raised. Avoid—at all costs—the fuzzy gray-green pallor of a peach picked prematurely. You should peel peaches before making jam of them. They're available all summer long.

The thing to look out for with cherries is mustiness. They break down quickly, especially when stored in plastic bags, where they readily develop off-flavors of the moldy variety. Dark cherry jam is lovely, but good sour pie cherries are the best thing ever. Sour cherries appear for a few brief weeks in early summer, but sweet cherries are available from late spring to late summer.

Your best bet for apricots are Blenheims. They should be velvety and maybe just a tad leathery-skinned for extra sweetness. Use your nose, not your eyes.

As we found out, even overripe blackberries make sturdy jam. They should have no trace of mold or rot, of course! If you're reasonably fit and live in the Pacific Northwest, you have no business buying blackberries. Bike out to your nearest thicket in August, roll down your sleeves, and watch out for snakes and turtles. Avoid berries near roads, as car fumes are foul-tasting and toxic.

Wild blueberries make exquisite jam, so seek them out if you can. Domesticated berries are marvelous, too, if you have a good source. Look for them in early to mid summer.

Plums make excellent jam, particularly the wickedly sour Damsons that grew behind our house. Good purple plums should be covered in a fine dusty powder (the "bloom," as in "the bloom of youth"). Yellow plums will make you a sparkly sunshiny jam. I find the modern hybrids—pluots and whatnots—rather gimmicky, not to mention bland and mealy. They're a mid-summer to autumn fruit.

Quinces were made for cooking, as anyone who has tried to eat one raw knows. They are chock-full of pectin, and will make an outstanding gel. It's dangerously easy to turn quince jam into quince paste, and dangerously easy to pair that paste with good cheese and gobble it up in one sitting. You'll find them in the fall and winter—they take on a creamy, golden color when ripe, and smell spicy and lemony.

Tender, seedy fruit like raspberries, wineberries, black raspberries, and the many varieties of each will make a seedy jam. I think that's just fine, but for seedlessness, make a jelly, and to dilute the seeds, make preserves or mix the berries with another fruit, like apples or peaches.

Apples keep so well in a cool cellar, and make such good cider and sauce, that I hardly think of preserving them with sugar. They contribute pectin and bulk to fruit combinations, and do make a very fine jelly. They're also a convenient canvas for spices, herbs, wines, liquors, honey, syrups, dried fruits, and other additions.

The best grapes for preserving are Concords, the purple autumn grapes that are largely descended from native North American species. Seedless table grapes make insipid preserves; wine grapes make distinctive preserves. Because of the seeds, most people make jelly of their grapes, but you can make jam if you put them through a food mill after cooking. Look for fragrant, firm, deeply colored, and slightly underripe grapes.

Firm, waxy cranberries are nearly foolproof. When cooked, they gel almost instantly. Unfortunately, their tartness can soak up a bundle of sugar—if you'd rather not get diabetes, try mixing them with apples and oranges for a nice little conserve. You can find them in the fall. If you get the chance, take a backpacking trip to a cranberry bog and spend a few days plucking them from their low, lacy foliage.

Pears can have a stringy, gritty, mushy quality in jam. I like them best as preserves (made like jam but with large, unmashed chunks of fruit) or jelly. Look for fresh pears in the fall, with dense, velvety flesh, a little tenderness to the touch, unwrinkled skin, and no bruising.

It's worth finding some unusual citrus fruits for your marmalade. Sour Seville oranges are the classic; bergamots are classy, and Meyer lemons so chic. Good citrus should be spicy and cleanly fragrant. They needn't be particularly ripe for marmalades. See Marmalade for specific instructions.

Persimmons of the soft, wild sort are useless unless fully ripe—and a good frost helps them ripen. In the markets you can also find luscious hachiya or crisp fuyu persimmons. Again, the hachiyas should be soft as a sack of jelly before you even think of eating them. They're a fall/winter fruit, and make a delicious (but quite brown) jam.

The tropical fruits strike me as more chutney-prone than anything—and for that purpose, are best in an underripe green state. Good mangos and papayas will still have a subtle fragrance when green—without any hint of grayness, mustiness, or refrigerated staleness.

Jam

First things first: Have ready some clean, sturdy little jelly jars, rubber-lined lids, and screw-on rings if you want to seal your jam. You can find canning jars and equipment in most hardware stores or supermarkets. Or have some little jars and kitchen wax/paraffin ready. Or have one big jar if you just want to use your jam fresh. Sterilize your jars, lids, and rings by putting them in a large pot of water and bringing it to a boil. Do not put glass jars in already boiling water—they can explode if their temperature changes too rapidly. Keep the jars warm in their water or in a 200-degree oven until you're ready to use them.

Rinse your fruit and trim it as necessary: cut out all bad spots, stems, pits, and cores. For the most delicate consistency, peel anything with a coarse skin. Pear and peach skins can get quite rubbery, but plum skins seldom prove a problem, provided they're chopped up. Grapes need their skins for color (see Grapes, above). Chop the fruit coarsely if it's large, and put it in a wide, heavy stainless-steel or enameled pot at least two times as large as the volume of fruit. You should only cook small batches of fruit at a time (no more than two quarts), as you want to bring it to a boil and evaporate the water as quickly as possible. Large quantities of fruit will require much more cooking time, and will lose precious flavor.

Put the fruit over pretty high heat (you can get away with a lot of flame if your pot is sufficiently heavy) and crush it as it heats. Squeeze in the juice of half a lemon for each quart of fruit. When the fruit has released plenty of juice, add the sugar.

The sugar problem always bothers me. The more sugar you add, the less likely you'll be to find mold—but the less potent your fruit flavor will be. You can use less sugar and process your jam jars in a boiling water bath to sterilize them, but then it's very easy to overcook the jam and have it turn hard. Equal parts sugar and (pre-cooked) fruit makes a stable, sterile jam, but I prefer half that quantity. So I either make a very small batch, pour it in a quart jar, and refrigerate it right away (where it keeps a good long while), or intentionally undercook the jam and sterilize the jars (see below). If you'd rather not use sugar, I'm extremely sympathetic. Honey works quite well, and of course contributes its own array of amazing flavors. If you'd rather it make a subtle contribution, pick a mild clover honey. Should you use less than one part sugar (or honey) to two parts fruit, you may have to overcook your jam to get it thick, and it will become gummy rather than gelled.

I'm somewhat skeptical of agave nectar and brown rice syrup, but go ahead if you must. You can't, however, produce any sort of gel with completely artificial sugars like aspartame and saccharin—the natural pectin in fruit requires sugar to make a gel. You can buy pectin that doesn't require sugar to gel. It comes with recipes. Sometimes it makes very good jam. It doesn't concern us here.

*You'll see both large and tiny bubbles as the jam
nears the end of its cooking time.*

Bring the fruit and sugar to full-bore rolling boil, and let it boil and boil, while you stir to make certain it doesn't burn. A gorgeous foam will form on the surface, through which the bubbles will burst, and an amazing aroma will fill your kitchen. The whole bubbling mass will rise in the pot (that's why you want such a large one), before it begins to reduce at all. Lift your spoon out of the pot and observe the consistency of the jam. Many old recipes talk about a Coated Spoon or a Sheeting Stage when the jelly is thick enough to roll off the spoon as a single mass—not a drippy trickle. Unfortunately, jam is lumpy enough that it won't ever make you a smooth sheet. And when, exactly, is a spoon coated? If you dip a spoon in water, it will come out wet—though I don't suppose anyone calls that coating. Picture your spoon dipping into a jar of heavy cream. Or real maple syrup. *That's* coating. And that's all you should look for—cook the jam beyond a good coating, and you'll wind up with fruit leather. Getting the Coated Spoon may take as long as half an hour, if you have a lot of fruit. If you will be processing your jam in the canner, keep to the cream side of the Coated Spoon, slightly thinner than the maple-syrup consistency.

Ladle the jam into its jars, wipe the rims with a clean rag dipped in the hot water, and cap with lids (using tongs!). If

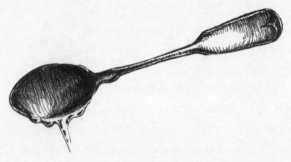

Jam will coat the spoon when it's done cooking.

the jam is not very sugary, you'll want to put the tightly lidded jars into the boiling water again and boil them for five minutes. Remove them immediately. Or just lid them and refrigerate. As the jars cool on the counter, the pressure inside the jars lowers until the lid seals with a joyful "pop!" A sealed lid will be slightly concave and taut; if you can pop the lid up and down, the seal is broken and the jam should not be eaten.

If your finished jam has the wrong consistency, you can always heat it up again and adjust it. Add water if it's too thick, or cook it longer if it's too thin. Of course, you'll likely imbue it with an overcooked flavor, but it won't be a disaster on your morning toast.

—R

Marmalade

The oldest marmalade recipes use honey, and the sharpness of citrus still stands up very well to honey's muting sweetness, whether or not we have access to refined, flavorless sugars.

Older recipes call for long waiting periods during the jam-making process—the idea being that you can extract a good deal of jelling pectin and soften the fruit during a long sit, without having to resort to as much boiling for the same effects. Softness isn't a particularly worrisome concern when dealing with, say, raspberries, but it can be problematic for tough citrus rinds. And yes, marmalade is more or less a jam of citrus *rinds*—the juice and pulp are nearly an annoyance.

The classic marmalade orange is the unpalatably sour Seville orange, which is full of seeds and can be rather dry. You don't have to have Sevilles for marmalade—sweet oranges, grapefruits, Meyer lemons, and bergamot oranges all make fantastic marmalade. Just avoid the seedless oranges and anything sweetly bland.

BASIC CITRUS MARMALADE

On the first day, take four large sour oranges and a lemon, wash them very well, cut them in half around the equator, and reach up inside their pockets to fish out all the seeds. For the most transparent marmalade, juice the fruit at this point and reserve, sieving out the pulp, and carving out and discarding the bitter pith from inside the rinds. Otherwise, just use the whole fruit. Save the seeds in a little dish. Cut the fruit into very thin, uniform slices or small dice—aesthetics can be your guide so long as each bit of orange or lemon cooks through as quickly as the next. Tie the seeds up in a scrap of cheesecloth and put all the fruit pieces, the seed-bag, and the juice in a bowl. Add four cups of water, push the fruit chunks and seed-bag under the surface of the liquid, and cover with a plate. Put it somewhere out of the way and leave it until tomorrow.

The next day, put everything in a nonreactive saucepan and bring to a boil. Reduce the heat and simmer until the rinds are quite tender and can be pierced easily with a fork. Pull out the seed-bag, let it cool for a minute, and squeeze the thick juice out of it back into the saucepan. You can get rid of the seeds now. Add a cup and a half of sugar or a cup and a quarter of honey. Bring to a rapid boil and cook until you achieve the Coated Spoon (see page 46). At this point you can let the jam sit again overnight, or jar it right away. Just bring it to a boil before you ladle it into sterilized jars and seal.

Root Cellar

To all you lonesome sighing darlings
you spinners in garrets
you scholars in towers
you martyrs on crosses
and children in attics

I say unto you:
it's all down in the cellar
better come on down
and come on down with
your rattling shoes your tattering coat
an old lover's booze and a dead lovenote
that sweet guitar and your silver spoon
(for peaches in jars hang fat as the moon).
Stoop through the lintel and stir up the air,
we're all going down in the harvest lair.

A hundred years ago, or four
(and she's lying 'neath the stones)
a woman raised her wooden spoon
and rattled her cold bones:
fetch me the red clay out in the pasture,
mine me the limestone out under the cows
build me a house like sweet vows and sunshine
frame it with great oaks and floor it with pines
but dig me a cellar way down in the mire
way deeper than snowdrifts; much deeper than fire
Houses may scorch and orchards shall burn
but the cellar, babe, must stand.
The cellar, babe, shall stand.

Was it Christmas, was it June?
A hundred years or four?
Sip your firewater,

watch the fire burn.
The oily tracks of smoke on plaster
add like sums you never learned,
and the starry little ashes
drift with snow across the porch.
Orchards scorch and barns blaze
but the cellar, babe, must stand.
The cellar, babe, shall stand.

Hey, old flame! It's a fine old game!
First you earn me, learn me, turn and burn me,
then I wine you, dine you—boil and brine you.
Yes, tune up your fiddle and trip down the stairs
get low on your knees and sing to the pears;
I'll show you where we bottle our hopes,
I'll show you how we seal up our cares,
I'll show you a summerlove any old time:
Since lovers are fickle, we learn how to pickle.

Kegs and caskets
crates and baskets
apples dry as liars' smiles
berries black and blue
cherries clotting dark and dense
ciders hard and true
plums like pouting lips
pursed for tater eyes
jealous green tomato relish
grapes for sour pies
cabbages—the mind you lost—
beets—the heart you stole
parsnips, prunes, and apricots
glassed away from mold
and peaches, peaches—sweet November!—
a-floating in my 'shine—
peaches, peaches—dear December!
sparkling in a line.

Oh, taste a summer five years old,
get your soul preserved,
spill your bottled old ambitions
shelved with love's munitions,
brush off the ashes, trip on down
—and when you trip on down,
bring your rattling shoes your tattering coat
an old lover's booze and a dead lovenote
that sweet guitar and your silver spoon
(for peaches in jars hang fat as the moon).
Shake down the spiders and shatter the plaster
rhyme me with limestone and uncork disaster
it's a root cellar—romp
it's a root cellar fruit cellar boot cellar stomp,
the house is on fire but the peaches are canned,
the house is on fire but the cellar shall stand.

—R

ALL THE OTHER MARMALADES

You can freely substitute your citrus and your sugar. Try four
large bergamot oranges and a cup of honey—that's my favorite.
Or use all Meyer lemons and put a bit of vanilla bean in each
jar when you're done. Try a cinnamon stick and a clove in with
the sour oranges when they're resting (take care with spices
that stay in the jar—they intensify over time). Chili peppers?
White peppercorns? Star anise? Whatever you like may go in,
but at a certain point you should call it chutney.

—R

Preserved Lemons

When life gives you lemons . . . make Moroccan Preserved Lemons. There is nothing to this at all. Just clean the lemons well—try to find organic ones or directly from a tree, because otherwise they'll be waxed. I use Meyer lemons from my backyard. Cut them into four quarters but leave the end intact so they stay whole. Sprinkle generously with salt. Start layering them in a jar, adding every now and then a stick of cinnamon, some cumin seeds, maybe a few chili flakes, and other spices you like, plus a pinch of sugar. When the jar is full, squeeze some more lemon juice on top so they are all submerged. Wait about a month. These are delicious with chicken, either as a condiment eaten peel and all, or cooked in a pan with chicken. You can also do this with limes, chopped roughly, and if you add some turmeric, fenugreek, coriander, cumin, a lot of chili flakes, and some oil, you get an Indian lime pickle, which is one of the most perfect foods on earth. It is exactly 100 times more interesting than hot sauce, with a hunk of lamb, even on a burger. I know, this veers perversely away from Indian tradition, but I feel the need to extol the virtues of this unsung beauty.

—K

Almonds

Some time ago, I was contacted by the local Almond Board to write about various subjects related to almonds—their transport eastward along the Silk Road, their use in Scandinavian cuisine and later in the Midwest, and finally a paper on the

European almond craze in the Middle Ages and Renaissance. There was such a craze, partly because almond milk and other products could be used during Lent and other fast days when meat and dairy products were forbidden. There was also a keen interest in almonds among physicians and dietary writers as an ideal health food, as well as remarkable creativity in cookbooks. The parallels to modern times are truly striking. In any case, I recovered many almond techniques that are well worth sharing, the majority of which have become completely extinct in the past few centuries.

ALMOND MILK

This is quite different from what can be bought in the store, normally sold for those with lactose intolerance, or vegans, next to the soy and rice milk. That stuff is sweetened and flavored with almond extract or some such other chemical. It may go nicely on cereal, but it is not medieval almond milk. For this you need raw almonds. Almonds are now always pasteurized to prevent E. coli, but for all practical if not philosophical purposes, they are still raw. These should be blanched. Until recently, I thought that meant a quick dip in boiling water to remove the skins. It does mean that today. But after reading the *Livre fort excellent de cuysine*, published in mid-16th-century France, I learned that blanching means a soak in fresh water for an entire day and night, which is essential to this recipe. Nothing more. Peel the almonds in the morning. This is time-consuming but not difficult. Please resist the urge to use ground almonds or toasted almonds. They just don't work.

Next, dry off the almonds and pound them in a mortar—a big one, ideally. Pound them all at once or in smaller batches, until it is a smooth paste. A blender definitely will not work. A food processor might, but we are not going there. Put the paste in a bowl and add a touch of sugar and salt. In the past, a dab of rosewater would go in, too. Why not? Over this pour warm water and let sit for about an hour, or if you're really patient, overnight. Then strain through a sieve or cheesecloth-lined colander. It looks and tastes like real milk and has exactly the same mouthfeel.

ALMOND BUTTER

Even more amazing is almond butter. This is not the ground-up almond spread that sits next to the peanut butter jars, or in the health food section of the supermarket. This is an entirely different product, and is literally butter made from almond milk. First you separate the fat from the water content in the milk. I have seen old recipes that call for vinegar, but it leaves the final product a little too sour, though they may actually have been looking for something like cultured butter. I recommend a little saffron in the milk to give the final product a yellowish hue. Rosewater, again, is up to you. I find that most modern diners, unless you're perhaps Moroccan, find the taste jarring. I like it. Either way, heat the milk gently until it starts to curdle and the solids begin to separate from the clear liquid, then pour it slowly into a fine cloth–lined sieve. A coffee filter works perfectly. The water will pass through the sieve, and in the filter you will have several spoonfuls of a soft, thick almond butter, which is as delicious as it is unctuous. Especially on bread.

—*K*

4
Grains and Pasta

I s there anything on earth as beautiful and comforting as a
forkful of elegant strands of fresh pasta, quivering in their
nakedness and tasting of nothing but noodle? There are
few foods as economical to make yourself—basically just flour,
water, and perhaps an egg and a pinch of salt. Dry pasta does
have its virtues: practical indestructability, a variety of entic-
ing shapes with ludicrous names. A decent brand of imported
pasta, a jar of sauce, maybe a sprinkle of dried herbs—this may
be all right, but it doesn't sing. It doesn't say to your family and
friends, "I applied a little elbow grease to these simple ingredients because I care about what you are eating—and you deserve
the effort." That's what fresh pasta says, loud and clear. When
matched with the right sauce, judiciously applied, the results
can be truly sublime.

First, one must abandon any notion that measurements
matter with pasta dough. They truly don't. If you want a lot
of pasta, use a lot of flour. If you want a couple of servings
use only a few handfuls. Nor do you need fancy equipment.
A rolling pin is just about it, but even that can be dispensed
with when making *orechiette* (little ears) or other hand-formed

shapes. Romantic cookbooks will tell you that *Nonna* poured her flour directly onto a wooden table and made a little volcano crater on the top (or *fontana*, as they say in Italian), broke in a couple of eggs, and slowly worked in the dough with a fork. This works with patience, but a big bowl is much easier to start with. Some sources will insist only a professional pasta lady with the nimblest of fingers and years of practice is allowed to touch the dough. Such people do exist in Italy, but they should not deter anyone from making pasta at home. I have seen young children make perfectly delicious pasta on the first try.

Basic Pasta Dough

To start, pour some flour in a bowl. All-purpose flour is fine, but avoid bread flour, which has too high a percentage of gluten—great for creating the tensile strength to hold air pockets in bread dough, but makes rolling out unleavened dough difficult. In Europe, the percentage of gluten in the flour is very low, especially in what they call "soft summer wheat." And making pasta there is actually physically easier because it has a lower percentage of those tough glutens. You can mix some pastry flour with regular flour for a similar effect. Or even buy Italian-type 00 flour, which is very finely milled and makes a pleasant soft dough.

Next break an egg in, or two. Or none. Or two yolks. It all depends on how eggy you like your pasta. I prefer one whole egg. Then add a pinch of salt and some water. *How much*, you ask? Enough to create a fairly stiff dough. Start by mixing the wet with the dry with a fork, and then switch to your hands. The dough should be pliable but not sticky. Move the dough to a wooden board and knead for about five minutes until smooth. You might need to add a little more flour to prevent it sticking, but try not to add too much. Now let the dough rest—in plastic wrap so it doesn't dry out, or under a bowl on the counter. Maybe an hour. Or not. Resting allows the glutens to relax and makes it easier to roll out. But if you're in a hurry, go right ahead and roll away. It will just take a little more oomph. This is your basic dough. Use it in all the recipes that follow.

Tagliatelle (with Tomato Sauce)

Go ahead and laugh, out loud if you must. But this is one of the most gorgeous combinations of ingredients on earth and I dare you to make it completely from scratch. I promise it will be a revelation.

Roll out your dough on a floured wooden board as thin as you like. I use a plain wooden pin without handles. Somehow I feel closer to the dough this way. An eighth of an inch seems about right. If making a lot, you'll need to do this in two or more batches. Cutting the noodles can be done with a sharp knife drawn along the edge of the rolling pin, or you can roll up the sheet and cut it with a scissor—but if the dough is even slightly wet, the noodles may stick together. Don't worry if they are not even and regular. Call them *maltagliati* ("badly cut"), and sound sophisticated.

There is also an ingenious device called a *cittara* (the words *zither* and *guitar* are both cognate). It is a box with metal wires tightly strung across either side. It doesn't sound too bad when strummed, either. You lay the sheet of dough on the wires and go over it with the rolling pin. Perfect strands fall into the box.

As with all cut noodles, a little flour on the dough will prevent them from sticking.

There are also pasta machines, not the electric kind—fie. I mean the hand-cranked models, which have been around for the past century. These are quick and produce a beautifully regular noodle, if that's what you're looking for. One end rolls out the pasta on successively narrower settings, so you can make absurdly thin dough. Start on the widest setting and feed the dough through a couple of times before changing the setting. Keep lightly flouring the sheet of dough as you go. The other side of the machine cuts the sheets into various widths, and there are also other attachments for ravioli and the like. I have been using the same pasta machine since I began to cook in earnest about 25 years ago, and have only had to replace the clamp that attaches to the table once.

I like to drape the fresh noodles over the backs of chairs or outside from a tree, only to admire the silken strands. Most people leave them in a clump; just be careful not to squeeze the clump, or they will stick. If you need to wait before cooking, put them in the fridge, covered with a towel—plastic wrap will cause moisture to condense on them and will ruin the lot.

When you are ready; that is, when your guests are ready to eat (pasta does not wait for people, people wait for pasta), have ready a big pot of salted water boiling rapidly. The *tagliatelle* will take about three minutes to cook, and you really mustn't boil them until the last minute. These are a little wider than linguine, and the wider the cut, the longer the noodles will take to cook. The only way to tell when it is done is to taste. You can throw it against the wall just for kicks, too. Serve with Fresh Tomato Sauce (page 23).

—*K*

A HISTORIC PASTA RECIPE

The marriage of pasta with tomatoes was not achieved until the 19th century. Even tomatoes themselves are not mentioned in Italian cookbooks until Antonio Latini's *Lo Scalco alla Moderna*, written in Naples at the very end of the 17th century, a full 200 years after Columbus. And his recipe was more of what we would call a chunky salsa than a properly cooked sauce. Before the popularity of the tomato, pasta was most often served with plenty of butter and a sprinkling of sugar and cinnamon. That was fairly typical of all dishes in the 16th century, and before you cringe, let me insist that you try it. The flavor of the pasta actually comes through much more clearly than with the assertive tomato. This recipe comes from a book written in Ferrara by Christoforo di Messisbugo, published in 1549, entitled *Banchetti*. Note that a standard pound was 12 ounces.

To Make Ten Plates of Maccheroni alla Napoletana

Take 8 pounds of finest flour, and the crumb of a large bread softened in rose water and four fresh eggs, and 4 ounces of sugar, and mix everything well together, and make your pasta. Remove a piece and of it make a sheet a little more thick than thin, and cut it into straight long strips, and repeat until all done. Then cook them in a good rich broth, boiling, and place them on your plates, or over capon or duck, or with sugar and cinnamon mixed in and on top, and for fish days cook them in water without butter. Or with good fresh butter if you want.

Buckwheat Noodles

Homemade pasta is a marvel of convenience—in fact, if you avoid clumsy, breakable pasta contraptions and their attendant set-up and clean-up times, noodles are easier than coconut balls or blondies or whatever else you made when you were 12.

"You rolled these all out without a pasta maker?" my boyfriend asked, incredulous and, I hoped, awestruck. "With*out* a pasta maker? Whatever do you mean?" I sniffed. "I *am* a pasta maker!" He's into pasta makers.

These are woodsy-flavored, lavender noodles, and would do very well with other sturdy flavors: in venison stroganoff, for instance, or in duck buckwheat noodle soup, or under a smoky peppery red sauce dolloped with sour cream.

Buckwheat isn't actually a grain, and has no gluten in it. That means the noodles are fragile, but not perilously so—my recipe uses half a cup of unbleached wheat flour for strength. You can go all-buck for gluten-free noodles with powerful flavor, wimpy structure, and beams of radiant good health.

In a mixing bowl, combine one and a half cups buckwheat flour, half a cup unbleached wheat flour, and two teaspoons salt and make a well in the center of the mixture. Add three eggs to the well, and whisk them vigorously, gradually incorporating all the flour. Dump onto a counter or tabletop and knead, wetting your hands occasionally, until pliable and smooth. Cover and let rest for at least half an hour.

Roll the dough on a well-floured surface until quite thin—a 16th of an inch or so. Cut into quarter- or half-inch strips and let dry while you take care of your water-boiling or soup-preparing duties. You might as well cut the strips into short pieces to pre-empt breakage. A pasta prenup, if you will.

Cook in well-salted boiling water or broth until thick, chewy, and cooked through—cooking time will depend on the thickness of your noodles, of course.

—*R*

Squash Ravioli

This is the one recipe most frequently requested by my wife. It is also among the most laborious I know, and cutting corners simply does not work. The most difficult part is surprisingly not filling the dough, but choosing and cooking the squash. I prefer to use Kabocha squash, grown by Mr. Nishi at my local farmers' market. They are dense and extremely heavy, and tinted so deep an orange color that your hands stain from cutting them up. And that is exactly what you'll need to do. Baking or microwaving just does not work. The trick is to cut the squash into wedges and then peel them with a peeler, or carefully cut off the skin with a knife. Roughly chop and put into a deep pot with a few knobs of butter, some salt, gratings of nutmeg, and a little water so they don't burn. Put on a low flame and cook for about 15 minutes until the squash is soft. Then mash and put on the lowest possible heat, uncovered, and cook another hour or more, stirring frequently, until you have a practically solid paste. The procedure is very much like making a roux. If you walk away, it burns—the Squash Gods, feeling neglected, will come and turn the heat up. So be patient. Set this paste aside and let cool; overnight in the fridge is fine, but you can use it the same day it's made.

Then roll out your sheets of pasta dough. For ravioli, you will want to cut circles with a glass or pastry cutter, put a dab of squash in the middle and cover with another circle, pressing out the air. The moisture of the squash will seal the dough; no need to use an egg wash. Or you can fold over each circle, making half-moons, or *agnolotti*. Or crimp the edges, or make tortellini, which involves filling half circles, then joining the ends, and flipping down the extra curved flap of dough. Place them on a floured tray to dry; uncovered is ideal, unless there are several hours before dinner, in which case, cover with a dishtowel. You can also cook them immediately if you're ready to eat. These will take only about three or four minutes to boil.

The traditional version puts amaretti cookies in the squash filling, and serves the ravioli with a *mostarda di frutta*—which is a lovely fruit preserve from Cremona and Mantua. You can buy this in a good Italian grocery store, or make your own. It's a lot like a chutney, oddly enough. The version from Mantua uses little candied sour apples and mustard essence. You can do it with crab apples and mustard powder along with other fruits (apples, peaches, apricots) cooked down with sugar until candied, syrupy, and thick.

Something a little tart works better as a sauce. Simply melt about half a stick of butter on low heat. Squeeze in the juice of one lemon. Add some capers; bits of raw or roasted pepper works nicely, too. Then at the last minute, off the flame, add a whole egg and whisk vigorously. If the sauce is too hot, the yolk will scramble. All you want it to do is thicken and enrich the sauce. Serve a handful of ravioli with a good drizzle of this sauce.

—K

Oatmeal Porridge

Sometimes I think that oatmeal is my favorite food, ever. I could eat oatmeal daily—several times daily—and be very happy indeed. Dr. Johnson would get up on his high horse (oat-fed, of course) and make snide comments, but frankly, oatmeal leaves me feeling competent and fortified, like I've swaddled my tummy in a hand-knit sweater and could take on a dozen old lexicographers.

But the oatmeal. Something as understated as oatmeal porridge has to be carefully crafted indeed if it's to compete with pretty little boxed cereals or hemp-infused granola.

The night before breakfasting on my favorite food, I soak one-third cup of rolled oats in a cup of liquid (water mixed with a splash of whey). The acidic bath improves the oats' complexion, makes them cook up quicker in the morning, and develops their flavor. Cover with a plate and leave somewhere warm to ferment. It's almost like breakfast is getting itself ready while you sleep. Almost like waking up to somebody else building the fire.

In the morning, add a little salt and cinnamon and bring the mixture to a simmer. Cover, turn off the heat, and let it sit until it's as thick as you like it. Sometimes I'll whisk in an egg when the oatmeal is thick but still hot, which makes it creamy-custardy. Actually, I confess I like to eat oatmeal when it's on the yonder side of lukewarm, springy-thick, and possibly even forgotten. Some like it cold. And when I drizzle it with blackstrap molasses, it sustains me for an entire morning.

—R

Flour Tortillas

Tortilla means quite a few things. I will restrict this to the Mexican unleavened flatbreads made of wheat or corn, though the eggy Spanish tortilla is certainly delicious.

Flour tortillas were born when the Spanish brought wheat flour to Mexico. They're the tortillas you use for burritos or just nibbling on with your supper. I learned how to make them from my housemate Mariza, who made them for almost every meal we shared.

Make the tortilla dough at least an hour in advance of when you want to cook them. It's just flour, butter, and water, so it keeps quite well for a day, well wrapped, in a cool room.

Put four cups flour and a little bit of salt in a bowl. An old variety of wheat, like spelt, works very well, but all-purpose or regular whole wheat or a mixture will do as well. With your clean fingers, work in half a cup of softened butter or lard. "You know it is ready and has enough butter if you can squeeze a handful of the flour/butter in your hand and then open your fist and find the mixture holds its form," says Mariza.

Next, slowly add a cup or so of water, kneading in between additions, until you have a fairly stiff dough. Keep kneading it until it's smooth and lifts the sticky bits of dough from your fingers. Wrap the dough well and let it sit on the counter until you're ready to roll it.

To roll the tortillas, flour the counter. Take an egg-size piece of dough and roll it to your desired thickness—between an eighth and a quarter of an inch.

Cook tortillas on a hot, ungreased griddle or tortilla plate. A dedicated cast-iron griddle is nice, but be warned that high heat without grease will destroy a cast-iron skillet's seasoning for other purposes. Cook it briefly on both sides until blistery and dry with darkened marks from the skillet. Keep cooked tortillas warm in a tea towel.

"You know you've mastered the skill if your tortilla bubbles up and becomes a 'tortuga,' or turtle, meaning that it all inflates and gets well cooked in the inside," Mariza says. "Tradition in my family is to eat the first tortilla with melted butter and salt; this one should be shared, of course . . ."

Corn Tortillas

Corn tortillas are the delicate, fragrant tortillas most commonly used for tacos. When cut into wedges and fried, they become tortilla chips. Before making corn tortillas, you first need to make masa, from nixtamalized corn. My friend Hannah grows the most beautiful blue field corn, which is perfect. Regular sweet corn will not do at all—buy a couple of pounds of large dried field-corn kernels.

Incidentally, pellagra—a crippling form of malnutrition rampant throughout the South a hundred years ago—could have been prevented if cooks had followed native tradition and nixtamalized their corn. Nixtamalization greatly increases the absorbable nutrient content of corn (notably, niacin) and improves its protein profile.

MAKING MASA

Soak two pounds of corn kernels overnight in an alkaline bath. Traditionally, ash was used as an alkalizing agent, but pickling lime works just as well. If you live near a Mexican market, you can find pickling lime quite easily under the name of "cal," short for calcium hydroxide. There is no substitute, but it is available online. Put half an inch of pickling lime in the bottom of a quart jar and fill the jar with water. Shake it well and let it stand overnight. The powder falls to the bottom, but the clear liquid is lime water. Pour it over your corn kernels—leaving the white sludge behind—and add more water to cover. Bring slowly to a boil, stirring occasionally, and let it boil for a couple of minutes. Turn off the heat, cover the pot, and let it sit overnight.

The next morning, rinse the corn under running water in a colander, rubbing it to loosen up the corn skins and discarding them. When well rinsed and de-skinned, grind the corn to a fine consistency. Because the corn has softened, this is not such a difficult task as it could be. You can pound it in a large mortar and pestle, if you don't happen to have the traditional masa-grinding *metate* made of lava rock. If you want to make very thin tortillas, grind it quite fine. If you want thick, moist, chewy ones, you don't have to work so hard. Freeze any ground masa you don't want to use immediately.

MAKING TORTILLAS

Knead a little water into the ground masa to make a soft, workable, not-sticky dough, and add a pinch of salt. You can also start with store-bought masa harina, which is masa that has been dehydrated. Use about three-quarters of a cup of water for each cup of dehydrated masa harina.

Let the dough rest for a while to absorb the moisture. Roll out egg-size pieces with a rolling pin on a lightly floured surface, or use a tortilla press. Hand-rolled tortillas will be less uniform and have some small cracks around the edges. Pinch large cracks back together, and consider adding more water.

Cook tortillas on an ungreased skillet. Cook the first side for less than a minute, just until the edges start to dry. Flip and cook until brown spots appear underneath. Flip and cook on the first side until similar brown spots appear. Keep finished tortillas wrapped together in a towel to stay warm and moist. Thin tortillas should only take a couple of minutes total to cook. Thicker tortillas will never get as dry as thin ones and should be cooked on lower heat for a longer time.

TORTILLA CHIPS

Cut a stack of thin corn tortillas in sixths and fry a few chips at a time in a couple of inches of hot lard or ghee until crisp. Drain on a rack and sprinkle with salt.

—R

Rice

The recipe I am about to share with you defies every rule you have ever read about cooking rice. The procedure requires no measuring, and may be used with any variety—fat *vialone nano*, slender delicate basmati, or ordinary long-grain rice. Put a glug of olive oil into a pan and add rice. However much you would like to eat, but don't fill the pan more than halfway because the rice expands dramatically. Crank up the heat and stir constantly with a close and watchful eye for about five minutes until the rice toasts a nice golden-brown hue. Note that this must happen before any other ingredients are added, or the rice won't brown.

Next add chopped onions, herbs, maybe saffron, and stir, until they, too, take on some color. The liquid in the onions will prevent the rice from getting darker. Add a pinch of salt and keep stirring. Then all at once add either water or good chicken broth (in which case, omit the salt). Stand back if you must, as the whole thing will splatter violently, which is half the fun. Pour in liquid about an inch above the level of the rice, give it a good stir, and turn the heat way down to low. Cover it and let it simmer gently for 20 minutes. Then turn off the heat and let it rest another 10 minutes or more before serving. Note, this is not a risotto; the grains are separate, firm, fully cooked through, not creamy. Technically, it is a pilaf.

The beauty of this recipe is that you can open up the pan to check the rice, add water, stir gently, but it requires no attention otherwise. You can also add other ingredients once the heat is lowered. Shellfish should go in about 10 minutes or less before the rice is done. Likewise, add fresh peas a few minutes before service. Chopped carrots should go in with the onion, as well as celery or peppers. You can add practically anything for a one-pan meal. Chopped ham, leftover chicken, string beans, or mushrooms are lush. Equally, the seasoning can be changed to match your mood: a fiery garam masala or curry; some soy, ginger, and garlic; a tomato-based *soffrito*, cooked separately and added toward the end of cooking. This dish is eminently adaptable to any flavor profile.

Risotto

Now, for the pure of heart, a risotto is something entirely other. You must use short-grain Arborio or similar Italian rice variety, so the tiny speck of starch remains toothsome in the center. Otherwise, the real difference is in the order of the procedure. Here, onions and flavorings are sauteed first, then the rice is added but will not brown. This is cooked slowly, uncovered, with increments of rich stock added ladle by ladle, the liquid only being added each time after the entire previous one has been absorbed. It also takes constant, methodical stirring. Getting the texture right—creamy and chewy at the same time—can be a little tricky, but not really difficult. At the end you hit it with a knob of butter and freshly grated real Parmigiano. Adding mushrooms makes this the classic Milanese version.

Paella

Paella is made much the same way, but you really need a paella pan—a big shallow pan with two little handles—set over a fire of grapevine cuttings. We tend to think paella must always include saffron, shrimp, and clams, Spanish chorizo and chicken, but actually there are many varieties, and I'm not convinced these ingredients aren't overpowered by the chorizo. Plain chicken breast is dreadful herein, but thighs with the skin on are really good.

In any case, one can do a paella of seafood alone: clams, shrimp, and scallops, all in their shells if possible, maybe with a few pieces of cod. It works nicely with a fish stock base, or even clam juice. Or use chicken alone with vegetables and chicken stock—which admittedly approaches the status of *arroz con pollo*. Rabbit and snails is a classic combination, too. Whatever you do, find good *Pimentón de la Vera*, a smoked Spanish paprika, which makes the dish sing.

Paella is cooked much like risotto, but you really don't want to be stirring it. Aficionados will tell you the best part is the crust that forms on the bottom of the pan. So do cook this gently and uncovered, without stirring, adding more broth now and then, until the grains are cooked through.

—K

5
Bread

There are many varied approaches to making bread. Some lucky few appear to have inherited a bread gene. They have a certain feel for the dough, and instinctively know how to nurture the living organism that is bread. Then there are those who approach baking as a science. I read a few recently published bread books before tackling this subject, and there is just no way I'm taking care of a starter like it was a pet, feeding it two or three times a day. I pored over the classics years ago, Bernard Clayton and James Beard in particular, as well as Gervase Markham from the 17th century. The older recipes are very imprecise, and the newer ones far too precise. Neither now nor when I first started baking have I ever been able to follow meticulous, exacting recipes. It is just not in my nature. I'd rather buy what I know is good bread from the pros than have to slavishly follow a complex recipe. I also have to admit that until recently, I never really adored the bread I made. And now I am so addicted that a corner of my kitchen is almost always occupied by a rising mound of dough, scattered drifts of flour, and a capacious bowl of starter (I will explain the simple magic of starter in a moment).

Before I delve into the wonders of wild yeast, allow me to offer some very simple observations about bread that hopefully will inspire you to dive into the dough without a recipe. Keep in mind, I never measure anything; my breads never turn out exactly the same twice, and I really like that. Consistency is overrated—I'd rather go for the really very good all the time, and the occasional exceptional accident that blows your mind, rather than follow a five-day, 20-page procedure that will frighten you away.

Also, remember that yeast is everywhere. On the flour, on your hands, in the air. It is not exactly wild though. That is, it has changed and evolved with humans and done marvelous things for us. But it is not as if it were unaffected by us, in a state of nature. There are hundreds of different species and varieties floating about. The stuff you buy in a packet should be thought of as industrial monoculture yeast, domesticated and bred for strength. It does a great job at making bread rise, but what you gain in speed you lose in flavor. Nonetheless, the packet need not be banished, and is a good place to start if you've never made bread before.

The easiest dough to start with, and one that can form the basis of many different doughs, is simple pizza dough. You will be amazed at how much better it is than the prebaked commercial crusts, and even better than most pizzeria crusts. No matter what anyone tells you, there is absolutely no reason *not* to make your own pizza dough. After a little practice, you will never go back. And when making this dough, trust your instincts. Somewhere in everyone there is a tiny dough gene inherited from our ancient ancestors. I have seen my students do this on the first try with very little instruction.

Pizza Dough

Take a packet of dry yeast. I prefer not the instant quick-rising type, but the regular kind, which needs to be proofed. Pour it into a big bowl and add a pinch of sugar. Pour over this a coffee mug (10 to 12 ounces) of 110-degree water. You don't have to take its temperature, just know that it's a little less hot than a cup of coffee. Not hot enough to scald you, which will kill the yeast, but not lukewarm, either. Leave it alone for about five minutes. You will see the yeast "bloom" and rise to the surface. I like to put my face right into the bowl and breath in deeply; it's magical. You can double the proportions if you want to make two pizzas in one batch. It's best to make a few batches if you want to more than double it; otherwise, you will need a positively monstrous mixing bowl.

Start pouring in unbleached bread flour while mixing with a fork. It will take about three cups. While mixing, add in a good pinch of salt. You can add a drizzle of olive oil to create a softer dough. You'll know you've added enough flour when the dough is no longer wet and sticky. Let it rest for a couple of minutes—or not, if you're impatient like me.

Take out a wooden board, flour it well, and start kneading. The trick to kneading is to fold the dough in half, press down with the heel of your dominant hand, give it a quarter-turn to the right, and repeat. Keep doing this, slapping the dough down on the board every few turns so you "wake the glutens." Glutens are protein chains that help create the pockets in dough that hold the gases that form during fermentation. After about 10 minutes, the dough should be springy and elastic; you'll probably have to keep adding a sprinkle of flour to the dough so it doesn't stick to your hands and the board. That's fine. You don't want to make it super-stiff, though a little sticky is okay.

Next, swish some oil into a clean bowl and plop in the dough, getting all sides oiled up a little. Put a kitchen towel over this and leave it alone for about an hour or two, depending on the temperature in the room. The colder it is, the longer it will take. If you want to make the dough some other time, pop it in the fridge covered with plastic wrap. It actually develops more complex flavors this way. Just bring it back to room temperature before baking. In either case, the dough will be about double in size.

Carefully turn out the dough onto a cutting board. You have two options here. If you have guts, flour your hands and drape the dough over the back of your hands with fingers pointing downward. With a quick rotation of your right hand toward you and your left hand away, you can toss the dough in the air. It is a lot of fun, providing you don't hit the ceiling. The object is to stretch the dough while leaving the edges fat for a crust, all while keeping the structure of holes inside the dough. When it's a nice pizza size, hopefully without any holes (which you can patch up with dough from the sides if necessary), put it on your peel dusted with cornmeal and add toppings. If you don't like cornmeal under your crust, you can also put the pizza onto parchment paper, which makes transfer into the oven a breeze. Slide it into a very hot oven (550 degrees), ideally onto a pizza stone that has been preheated in the oven. I have gone through two or three stones in the past 20 years, and my most recent cracked and was just replaced with a $12 stone. Works great. Cook until it is pizza with slightly browned crust and bubbling toppings. The time all depends on your oven.

If you don't have a peel and stone and don't feel like theatrics, here's an easier way to do it. Roll out the risen dough into a thin pizza shape and put it on a lightly oiled baking sheet without edges. With this one it's best to let it rise again for half an hour or more before putting on your toppings and baking, since the rolling usually breaks many of the air bubbles. This one is less likely to tear, and you can put the baking sheet directly into the oven without a peel or stone. If you like, you can slide the pizza directly onto the oven rack to crisp up for the final minute or so.

Pizza Margherita

If you are lucky enough to have a nice thin crust, the best approach is the classic Pizza Margherita, said to have been invented by Rafaelle Esposito for Queen Margherita of Savoy in 1889. I love the pizza in Italy—the spare toppings, the cracker-like crust. It's just a different creature than what we call pizza in this country. For the classic, you do need a peel, and stone, or better yet, a wood-burning oven. Without one of those, crank your oven up to 550 degrees or as hot as it will go. Even 800 degrees would be fine. Just before baking, I like to throw an ice cube in the oven to create some steam; it gives the dough a lift, and is a good practice for all bread baking. Some people spray the oven with a mister, others put in a ramekin of hot water. All of these are fine.

On the peel, top your pizza dough with a ladle of tomato sauce, swirled in a spiral, which leaves an exposed swirl. If you put on too much sauce, you will have the "pizza slide" when the toppings come off. Not really an insurmountable problem if the pizza is eaten on a plate with a fork and knife as they do in Italy, but still, unpleasant. Then top with a scant handful of shredded mozarella scattered, though to be authentic it should be a few slices of *mozarella di buffala* just placed on the sauce swirl. Then add a few basil leaves. That's it. Slide it into the oven. It should take only a couple of minutes. In Italy people often add a drizzle of olive oil when it comes to the table, with good reason, since the pizza is usually a bit dry. A little sea salt and freshly ground pepper won't hurt either, but that's it. This is the pristine Ideal Platonic Form of Pizza. A touch of prosciutto is allowed, or a few anchovies, but it must be spare, thin, a little burnt on the edges, and should mostly taste of bread, not sauce and cheese.

American Pizza

As an adoptive Californian, I can venture forward with you on a more adventuresome pizza. Start with your dough on the thicker side. I am unorthodox (some would say heretical) in my approach to building a pizza. I start with mozzarella, torn by hand into small chunks and scattered on the surface. Liberally. Sometimes I toss the cheese with a bit of grated Parmigiano-Reggiano first (please, the real stuff.). Then I plop little dabs of sauce all over the surface, using a spoon. I use a rich sauce with onions and lots of herbs, more like a thick marinara than a thin pizza sauce. Then on top, put whatever you like. My kids prefer pepperoni. My current favorite is sauteed broccoli rabe and walnuts, with a little chèvre. Maybe a few mushrooms or capers. Or caramelized onions or shallots if they're not already in the sauce. Literally, anything you like goes. Try to bury the nuts so they don't burn, especially pine nuts, but otherwise, the possibilities are unlimited. Of course sausages and peppers are classic, as are clams and white sauce, though I'm the only one who will eat that. I spent a year in New Haven and after eating the perfect white clam pizza at Sally's, I swore I would learn to do it. That was more than 20 years ago.

After your toppings are on and you've slid your pizza onto the stone, cook the pizza full blast, with an ice cube tossed straight on the oven floor, for about 10 minutes, or until it looks like a cooked pizza. I usually leave it until the crust is brown, but slightly golden works, too, depending on how you like it. A few gratings of Parmigiano-Reggiano on top before service is wondrous. Cut this pizza into wedges and eat it with your hands.

Pita Bread

This same pizza dough makes excellent Indian *naan* as well as flour tortillas, pita bread, and any flatbread you like. Pinch off knobs and roll them into balls firmly between the palms of your hands, creating a little spiral in the dough. Then, with the spiral upward, roll them out flat on your dusted board and set aside on another floured surface. In this case, you're not worrying about an airy light texture, though it will get a little rise when cooked. You can put these rounds in the oven and bake them, which is easiest. But I find using a stovetop flame is a lot more satisfying.

You can start cooking each round of dough in a very hot nonstick pan, cooking on each side for about 30 seconds, then transfer it directly to the open flame of a burner with tongs (or your fingers, if you're crazy like me) for a few seconds on each side. If you are lucky, the steam inside will cause them to inflate, creating a pocket. You can also press on the top with a kitchen towel gently to encourage the steam to open the entire flatbread. They char a little, which gives them incomparable flavor and texture. For the adventurous, cook them right on the barbecue on low heat, being careful not to let them burn. For the truly, truly adventurous, use a clay tandoor oven, with a charcoal fire in the bottom. The dough is slapped on the side walls while meat and vegetables roast on skewers that are vertically arranged down the center. This is a thing of great beauty.

Take each cooked pita (however you do it) and put them in a covered container, or on a big plate with another plate inverted on top. This keeps them warm and steams them a bit. Continue until all the dough is used up. They will stay fresh, covered, for several hours. You will be amazed at how much better this is than commercial pita, even if you don't get a pocket. The texture is chewy and it is very hard to stop at one, especially with a scoop of hummus or *baba ganoush*. Or you can make little individual pizzas out of them, roll them around fillings for burritos, and even bake them in a casserole filled and covered with sauce and cheese. They are eminently adaptable to any recipe that requires flatbread.

—K

Challah

I make challah exactly once a year: on Rosh Hashana. I am often told that it is infinitely superior to those you can buy in the store, and I have to agree. The recipe can also be used to make any eggy bread. Call it what you will: Easter Bread with a red hard-boiled egg in the middle if you're Greek, brioche if you're French. Okay, this is not real brioche, but it tastes really good.

Start exactly as with pizza dough, but this time with two packets of yeast, proofed with sugar and two mugs of 110-degree water. To this, add a good pinch of crumbled saffron threads. I love the color and the medicinal flavor. The whole thing will turn bright yellow. Then add about a quarter pound of honey—that's a quarter of a standard pound jar—or you can use as much as half. It will obviously be a sweeter bread, which for Rosh Hashana is traditional. Then add two whole eggs, some salt, and about a quarter cup of vegetable oil. You can use melted butter if you want to approximate brioche. This will take a lot more flour than the pizza dough because of the added liquid. Don't worry, just keep adding until you have a dough. Knead just like before, and let rise like before.

The only major difference here is that you will punch down the risen dough, form the challah, and give it a second rising. Forming the challah is exactly like braiding hair. You can make one very big bread out of this, or two smaller ones. The basic method is the same. Divide dough into three balls and with both hands roll out into a long snake. You can swing them around and over your head to stretch out. Make them as long as you can, but be sure not to flatten or squash out the air pockets. Then take the three strands and braid them, tucking in the loose ends. Put this bread on a baking sheet, and let it rise again until doubled in bulk. Brush gently with a whole egg and bake at 350 degrees until golden brown. Let cool uncovered before you dig in, but do wrap it up after cooled. You can add raisins to this, and nuts if you like, but I prefer it plain and straight and a little less sweet. Slathered with butter, or drizzled with honey, it is an excellent way to start a new year.

CHALLAH FRENCH TOAST

The apotheosis of this bread, I must tell you, is French toast. Slice the challah and leave it out a day or so until dry. Then mix up some eggs, milk, a grating of nutmeg, a sprinkle of cinnamon, some salt, and plenty of pepper. Then soak the dry bread in the mixture as long as you can, even overnight in the fridge. Put each slice carefully into a hot pan with plenty of melted butter. Press some crushed pecans into the upper surface and scatter some sliced apples (the tarter the better), around the French toast while still in the pan. Probably two slices per pan is best. Flip over and cook on the nut side; they should stay embedded. After a few minutes, invert onto a plate and serve with the apples on the side and a drizzle of real maple syrup, warmed. A dollop of sour cream, too. You could *plotz*.

—*K*

Sprouted Grain Bread

The ancients sure knew how to be lazy. So much of their arduous labor required a moment of planning and a lot of sitting around. I put a bunch of enzymes to work three days ago. They've been slaving away for me in my kitchen, spinning starch into sugar, and now I am about to eat their delicious bread.

I first made sprouted wheat bread one fall when I needed something besides cranberries to sustain myself on a cranberry-picking backpacking trip. Its dense texture—caramelized crust and moist interior—utterly enchanted me, especially paired with the crotchety old Cheddar I'd packed along.

The process is simple. Soak wheat berries (soft white, hard red, spelt, or kamut) one morning in plenty of filtered water. At nightfall, rinse and drain them. You can leave them in the bowl, but be sure they're well enough drained that water isn't pooling in the bottom. Depending on the temperature of your kitchen, they might have little sprouts the next morning or evening, or even later. Rinse and drain them twice a day for as long as it takes them to sprout—cheesecloth rubber-banded to the rim of your bowl or crock makes the draining much easier. The white sprout should be about one-third the length of the grain, but don't be fooled by the skinny little rootlets, which are longer and wigglier than the true sprout. If the berries sprout too much, the enzymes will eat all the starch and turn it into sugar—and good luck making bread from pure sugar. If they don't sprout enough, the bread will not be magic.

Once they are perfect, put them through a meat grinder. I like to add some dates (pitted, please) while I'm grinding—about half a cup per pint of sprouts—and I think a hand-cranked meat grinder is the best tool for the task. A sufficiently large mortar and pestle is quite effective in strong and patient hands, but an electric meat grinder may heat things up too much, and the hand-cranked ones are much easier to find in that thrift-store bin. You'll have to grind the whole mess several times over; the more consistent the texture, the better your bread shall be. Keep in mind that after their time in the oven, any little unmashed pieces of the grain will be hard enough to crack teeth.

After several passes through the grinder, the mashed wheat berries will become a cohesive dough. As they soaked and sprouted, they absorbed all the water necessary for making dough—resist the temptation to add any more. Once the dough has been ground to a smooth and relatively even consistency, knead the sticky mess and let it sit for a while. Of course, it isn't going to rise, but because it's so full of magic germinating energy, and *might* catch some wild yeast from the air, I do let it rest. Anyhow, gluten always likes beauty rests to stay strong and elastic.

I shape the dough into little oblong loaves, maybe two inches tall and the size of my hand with my thumb tucked under, and let the loaves sit a bit before slashing them thrice with a sharp knife and putting them in a slow oven (between 250 and 300 degrees) for a couple of hours. Don't be surprised when they rise in spite of the complete absence of leavening agents. It's just steam—add a few pistons and you've got the industrial revolution. When your whole house smells like honey and hay, and the loaves are crusty and deeply colored, you may pull them from the oven. They soften up if you wrap them and store them somewhere cool for several days, but I don't know anybody who can resist fresh bread.

On a hot, dry day, you can also bake them in the sun. Instead of loaves, make little rounds about half an inch tall and three inches across. Choose the hottest spot, and set up a screen or old window if they are in danger of getting dirty junk blown on them. Put them out in the morning, flip them at noon, and let them go till sundown, or whenever they are all dried out. They will puff and darken, but won't be as caramelized as they get in the oven.

—R

Sourdough Bread

It isn't, I think, any sort of accident that ancient brewers and bakers used to call their sourdoughs "goddisgoode." Old-fashioned long-fermented sourdough bread has several distinct advantages over quick-risen bread made with commercial yeast. The crust, for one, is chewier and more satisfying, the bread has deeper flavors, and the loaf itself stays moister much longer. Even better, the long fermentation allows the grain more time
to break down before
baking, making the
grain's nutrients
more available
to the body.

CATCHING YOUR YEAST

Here is where baking begins to get really thrilling. Buckle up. After reading some acclaimed sourdough recipes by master bakers, some that took a full two weeks to get started and thrice-daily feedings, I was about to lose heart. Then I recalled my general approach to cooking. Wing it. A few hundred years ago, no one had lengthy recipes like these; they usually learned from elders. Why couldn't I at least give it a shot? It is not a baking gene with which some lucky few are born, but simple knack and guts. Exactly everything that had eluded me thus far in bread making was suddenly right there in front of me. Let me explain.

Wild yeasts, or let's say ambient yeasts, are quite different from commercial bread yeast or *Saccharomyces cerevisiae*, literally "sugary fungus of beer." The wild guys are sometimes a different species altogether, for example, in San Francisco it's *S. exiguus*, which apparently only thrives in the cold fog, just 90 miles from my house, but a completely different climate. Here it is blazing hot, usually still in the 90s in late September. This year, we had a strange summer and the grapes ripened really early, then all at once the weather changed, down in the 70s on October 1, with rain in the forecast. So I thought, time to catch some wild yeast.

This is the simplest thing to do. Put out some food, and the babies find it. They like to eat flour. Simple as that. They're also usually already on the flour you buy. If you have some grapes around, the powdery stuff on the outside is exactly what you're looking for; that's yeast. You can chuck the grapes into a flour-and-water slurry and let them go. Whole wheat flour works well, and rye even better. You can use both. Raisins work fine, too. Let the flour, water, and fruit, if using, sit outside or on the counter uncovered for a day. On the second day, cover loosely with a kitchen towel, but never seal with plastic wrap, which prevents the living yeast from breathing.

From this point on, it is only a matter of regular feeding. On the second day, feed the barm (as it is traditionally called in England) about a cup each of unbleached bread flour and water, stir, and leave it alone. On the third day, add flour and water again, a little more than before. Feed it every day. If you don't, the alcohol produced as the yeast gobbles up the sugars (which come from the broken-down carbs) overwhelms the yeast and bacteria. The bacteria are what give the bread its sour bite. You want both of them to be happy. And there is no reason to put it in the fridge, since we are going for antique methods. All this means is you have to use some every day, give some away, or toss a little in the trash. Heaven forfend!

After about a week, your starter may be ready to go. My first was ready on October 4, 2008, and was named Durga after the Hindu goddess whose name means "unfathomable" female principle of unforgiving rage and enduring, endless love. This was her day.

Wild Yeast Bread

Make your bread with a cup of starter, a cup of water, a pinch of salt, and enough flour for a firm dough. Knead for a good 10 minutes, then let rise for about two hours. Knock down the dough and then form into a Pugliese shape, sort of like a football. Let it rise a second time for about three hours covered with a dishcloth, then slash it two or three times diagonally with a sharp knife just before baking.

The key is in the baking. Crank up the oven to 550 degrees, or as high as it goes. Throw a couple of ice cubes onto the oven floor, and let the steam build up. Transfer your dough gently to the peel. Then slide in the bread onto a preheated pizza stone. You will see the thing rise to nearly double in volume, bursting out of the slashes. It will take maybe 20 to 25 minutes until it is deep brown and sounds hollow when thumped. Let it cool on a rack for a few hours, then slice it.

The crumb on my first loaf was a little dense, and clearly Durga was still a little young and weak. But the crust was absolutely phenomenal: thick, crusty, chewy, all at the same time. It was a revelation. Everything I had been looking for in bread.

LARGER SOURDOUGH *BOULES* AND OTHER SHAPES

After a few weeks, your starter will be powerful and will smell like yogurt. At this point you can go for bigger, more interesting shapes. Begin with a cup of starter, two cups of water, and about seven cups of flour. This will take about four hours to rise the first time, though it really depends on the temperature in your kitchen.

Once it rises, punch down and work the dough into a round shape by rolling under the edges so that the upper surface is taut and slick, and let rise another two and a half hours. At this point, you can cut a circle from the center with a cookie cutter, giving you a shape like a huge bagel, the sort of Italian breads I used to buy in the Bronx. The "hole" can be baked separately as a roll, too. Or, you can divide the entire bread into little rolls, which come out super-crisp and chewy. Two long thin baguettes are also an option. For a cleaner line and better expansion, try snipping them with a scissor rather than slashing with a knife. Or you can bake the round as is, a big sourdough *boule*. If you are having trouble with the bread rising, you can add a pinch of commercial yeast to the dough, just for some extra lift. But don't put it in your starter or it will probably dominate the native yeasts.

Here's what eventually happens: You get into a rhythm of feeding the starter, every day, or even every other day—there is no need to be uptight about this—by just plopping in a bit of flour and water and stirring it up. I have found that baking is best a full 8 to 12 hours after feeding, when the bubbles and lifting power are strongest. There is also absolutely no need whatsoever to put your starter in the fridge—unless maybe you're going away. Even then, let a friend mind it. I have kept Durga right on the counter for months and she is perfectly happy. I have also gotten in the habit of baking maybe twice a week, and I am now convinced that the bread is better than anything that can be purchased. Even my favorite store-bought ciabatta tastes flat now.

As it gets colder, the yeast gets sluggish and needs more time to rise. This turns out to be a good thing. In a cold December kitchen, I make the dough one day and leave it out all night to bake first thing in the morning. Resist using any commercial yeast—it's a shortcut for which you will sacrifice flavor, and if you leave it too long, it will overferment and taste unpleasant.

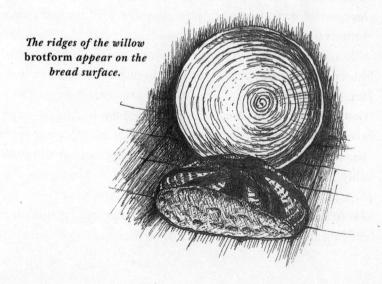

The ridges of the willow **brotform** *appear on the bread surface.*

If you can let the dough rise in a willow *brotform*, as it's called in German, all the better. This is a spiraled basket thing, which you flour, then plop the dough in after its first rise, cover it with a towel, and let rise a second time. Don't worry if the dough doesn't look like it has risen twice in volume; most of the rising happens in the oven with the initial blast of heat. The basket also lets the dough surface dry out slightly so that when it is slashed the dough doesn't pull and deflate. After you turn it out onto a floured peel, slash the top deeply into a star pattern with an X-acto or really sharp knife. (I bought a French contraption, a curved razor on a stick, for $25—but it doesn't work as well.) These slashes will open up while baking, but the spiral pattern stays there as well. It is absolutely breathtaking to behold, and delicious as well. I also tried the perforated metal baguette forms, which leave little dots on the bottom like you see on commercial French bread. I prefer the stone, and I think it is absolutely essential to a good lift in the oven. As an experiment, I made one loaf on the stone and another on a baking sheet—same dough, temperature, and steam in the oven. One sprung up beautifully; the other was flattish and dense.

Some other observations: the flour really does make a difference. It must be bread flour with high protein content, and I have always had better results with organic flour. But beyond this, do play with various combinations of flour. Half dark rye flour, in which case don't knead the bread. It needs a longer rise, yields a gorgeously dense, seriously sour bread, the like of which I have not tasted since spending the summer doing research in northern Germany. A bit of graham flour or whole wheat flour improves the taste and texture a lot. Spelt is also really tasty.

Most important, with bread baking, you have to accept inconsistencies. Every now and then something will go wrong. The dough will be accidentally deflated, will stick to the bowl, will come out too dense, or may overferment. That's fine. If you want exactly the same thing every time, you might as well buy it at the store. But life is so much more interesting with surprises—usually good ones.

And should you, dear friend, at some point become neglectful of your sweet, hard-working starter and forget to feed her, for perhaps a week, and upon your return find her stinking to high heaven? Yes, she is dead. But no worry, there is still yeast all over the place. Pour this starter out, clean the bowl, and put in more flour and water, feed regularly, and within two weeks you will have offspring ready to do some serious lifting.

—*K*

Wholemeal Bread

This is a good bread for the peasants—a hunk of crust to sop up your supper. You'll want to start by building yourself a rye sour. Rye ferments magically—even if you want a wheaten loaf, you should make a rye sour. If you've had trouble making yeast-leavened rye breads in the past, you should try sourdough ryes. Rye flour lacks the high gluten content of wheat, and sometimes makes a weak, puddly loaf, but it performs much better when allowed to ferment slowly.

RYE SOUR

Mix a pint of fresh dark rye flour and a pint of water. Put it on the counter, loosely covered. The next morning, add a cup of rye flour and a cup of water. Continue adding flour and water daily, transferring the sour to a clean bowl every other day or so to keep crusty build-up from growing mold. Within a few days, the mix should turn sour and bubbly. If it doesn't, throw it to the hogs and start again. There are billions of hungry yeasts and bacteria in your kitchen that would love nothing more than a good bowl of flour and water. They can't avoid temptation indefinitely—sooner or later, you'll find some grateful yeasts. After a week of successful souring, you can try baking with the starter. Continue feeding it daily. A day or two of neglect is not a huge problem, so long as you keep it well fed for a few days before you plan to bake. Skim off any odd-looking scum that might form on top.

A note on the freshness of flour: Once whole grains are ground into flour, they oxidize rapidly, and the fats in them go rancid. In fact, most people who object to whole grains object to the off-flavor of *rancid* whole grain. While saving up for a good grain mill, I keep my wholegrain flours in the freezer.

Feed the sour the night before you plan to bake. The next morning, mix a quart of sour with a tablespoon of salt in a large bowl and stir well. Add six cups fresh wholegrain flour (rye, wheat, spelt, or kamut), and stir with a hefty wooden spoon. The dough will no doubt be too stiff, so work in a cup or more of warm water as you knead. The moisture level of whole grain flour can vary so much that precise measurements are down-right deceptive. If you pick up a fist-size chunk of dough, it shouldn't give you much resistance when you pinch through the middle of it. The wetter your dough, the holier and chewier your bread will be—up to a point, of course.

Even whole-grain dough will be supple and stretchy when well kneaded.

There are many ways to knead dough, but the main idea is to efficiently agitate the whole mass without ripping it. I rapidly lift the dough on the side opposite me and push it into the middle, rotating the bowl a bit with each fold. The dough will grow less sticky as you knead—but if it sticks too much, wash your hands. (Dough doesn't stick very well to clean, wet hands.) You can also knead on a clean tabletop (but that usually requires flour), or push a stool up to the counter and knead there, so long as you maintain a height advantage. When you can see long strands in the dough, and it looks quite smooth and silky, turn it smooth-side up, cover the bowl with a tea towel, and leave it in a warm spot. Let it take its time rising—it can double its size in four to eight hours. To tell if it is ready, poke the dough with a wet finger. If the hole doesn't fill in at all, gently push the dough down, knead it briefly, and let it rise as before. This second rise should take less time.

Once it's risen twice, scoop or push the dough out onto a well-floured surface and swiftly form it into loaves. If you don't have a baking stone and peel (which I heartily recommend), just place the loaves on greased baking sheets or in loaf pans. Two longish loaves work well, or one loaf pan and a smaller loaf.

Cover the loaves with a tea towel and let them rise again until soft. Test them by licking your finger and poking the dough gently, up to the base of your fingernail. When the dough very slowly fills in the dent you made, it's ready to bake. This may take a couple of hours or more.

Get the oven really, really hot—most ovens max out at 550, but try it hotter if yours can do it. Brush the loaves with water (or delicately spread it with your fingers) and slash them with a very sharp knife or razor. Pop them in the oven. A few minutes later, quickly open the oven door and throw more water on them—or ice cubes on the oven floor. Depending on their size, they may take 30 to 45 minutes to bake. Let the temperature fall toward the end of baking, especially for the larger, more compact loaves. You can reduce it to 350 degrees or simply turn off the oven, if it holds heat well. When they are nicely burnished and make a hollow sound when thumped, pull them out of the oven. Be sure to let them cool thoroughly before wrapping them for storage. Whole-grain loaves keep best in the refrigerator or a cool room.

Note: If you neglected your sour the day before baking, make a sponge first thing in the morning: Mix two cups sour with two cups each water and flour, stir thoroughly, cover, and leave in a warm, sheltered spot for three to four hours. Once it forgives you and bubbles up, add flour, salt, and water, and proceed as usual.

—R

Sourdough Herb Muffins

These are a crusty, moist quick treat. The sour makes them taste remarkably cheesy.

Mince a few twigs' worth of fresh rosemary and oregano, and whisk with half a cup white flour, half a teaspoon baking soda, two teaspoons salt, two tablespoons sugar, and a quarter cup oat bran.

Add one and a half cups sourdough starter, one egg, three tablespoons melted butter, and two to three tablespoons whey, buttermilk, or sour milk. Whisk briefly, pour into a greased 12-muffin pan, and bake at 350 degrees until golden.

6
Meat

The shift to hunting and meat eating played a central role in human evolution, bringing us out of the forest and into the open plains, forcing us to stand upright, to run swiftly, and to cooperate in larger social groups. The domestication of animals ten thousand years ago, along with cereals, brought us into more permanent settlements, and led to what we now call civilization. Whether the taste for meat is therefore programmed into our bodies, we will not venture to guess, but we assure you these recipes satisfy some primal part of the brain, especially since they use ancient techniques. Feel free to don a loincloth while preparing any of these.

The Gentle Art of Roasting

All you really need to start roasting is a hunk of meat, an open fire, and a long metal pole with a crank on the end or even a spear of fresh green wood. Keep in mind, you do need actual fire to roast—an oven simply won't do. But there are civilized ways to roast. One of the most exciting things I have ever purchased is a clockwork turnspit. It is a little metal box made in Italy based on a 19th-century design, sold in this country by spitjack.com, though there are other commercial models available online. Mine has two spits that connect to the box and comes with adjustable pins that go both into the meat and fasten to the spit so the food doesn't flop around while turning. A hand-cranked spit also works fine, and you can make one, too. All you need is an iron rod and a friend with an acetylene torch. You will need to bend one end into a handle and sharpen the other into a point. Then weld two fork tines like a trident in the middle of the rod to hold the meat in place.

Tie the lamb securely on a turnspit and roast beside the fire, over a drip pan.

To use a spit, just put a chicken or duck or even a small turkey onto the spit, pierced through the flesh at either end. If the bird is at a slight angle with the breast facing away on each orbit, the breast will not overcook while the legs are cooking through. A 10-pound tied roast beef works wonderfully, too. If you are a hunter or have hunting friends, do try a leg of venison, best larded with strips of fat. Even a bear leg is wonderful and juicy, and if you are lucky, the fat will taste of the berries the bear has been eating.

The technique: First make a serious fire in the fireplace, or even outdoors on the ground surrounded by rocks or bricks. Set up the spit *next* to the fire. It should not be over the flame or it will burn. That's precisely what makes roasting so much more interesting and easier than grilling. Under the spit, put a pan to catch the drippings. If you're using a clockwork turn-spit, the mechanism turns the spit slowly for about 15 minutes when you wind it up, and then rings when nearing the end. Just wind it up again. If you have a manual transmission spit, just keep turning it slowly without stopping. You'll need to turn the crank by hand for a few hours without stopping, but it's so nice on a cold day. And at the end you have a beautiful, evenly browned, juicy roast. Not a crispy top and soggy bottom, like you get using an oven. The juices for the most part stay inside the roast, so don't expect cupfuls of drippings for gravy. I honestly think this is why in the past they made sauces out of something other than drippings. And frankly, I think the idea of letting all the juices drip out and then making a sauce from them is just a bad way to cover up dry meat. Keep it in the roast, and it hardly needs sauce.

Roast Piggie

To roast pig in an indoor fireplace, use a very young suckling pig, no more than 15 pounds or so. A larger pig should have a long spit of about six feet, set beside a fire made directly on the ground or in a pit. A 30-pound pig is of manageable size, and will easily feed 20 people. A 30- or 40-pounder can also be cooked in an oven, and will take roughly four hours at this size. Think of it as a very large turkey, to which in taste it largely resembles at this age. Just keep in mind that cooking it in an oven will not give the benefit of proper roasting by a flame: crackling skin and unctuous flesh.

First, marinate your whole pig overnight. A combination of oil, vinegar, mustard, and garlic, plus herbs such as sage and thyme works nicely. So, too, does a Mexican combination of lime juice, chilies, cilantro, cumin, and oregano with a bottle of beer, or better yet a good splash of tequila. Thread it on the spit and roast until crackling brown, and the juices run clear when pierced with a knife. The time will depend on the temperature of your fire, but four or five hours should be fine for a 15-pounder. A 30- or 40-pound pig will take more like seven hours, but it all depends on the heat of the fire, the shape of the fireplace, and other variable factors.

Present the whole pig at table and carve by first removing the legs, and then slice thin pieces from the shoulder, loin, and rear legs. The crunchy ears are delightful, and as Colin Mackenzie's *Five Thousand Receipts in All the Domestic and Useful Arts* (1829) says, "Some are fond of an ear, and others a chap, and those persons may readily be gratified." The chap is the pig's cheek, as in Bath Chaps, which are cured and smoked like bacon. Think of that the next time you describe a friend as a nice chap.

—*K*

Braised Game or Offal

When someone hands you a chunk of game, chances are good you should braise it. Wild, happy animals frolic too much to be consistently tender, but a thorough braise will soften all their tough muscle fibers. If you're not sure how tender the meat is,

MEDIEVAL PIG RECIPE

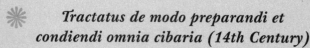

Tractatus de modo preparandi et condiendi omnia cibaria (14th Century)

TRACT ON THE WAY TO PREPARE AND SEASON ALL FOODS

"A young little pig in truth roast whole, don't cut off the feet or head, and fill his body with aromatics tied up with his liver, and roast; with a spit pierced through transversely, first through the shanks and head; and for eating serve with a pepper broth or cameline sauce. Because it is a phlegmatic food and corruptible in the stomach, hence accompany with good condiments."

The nutritional advice tagged onto this recipe suggests that pork, because categorized in the medical system of humoral physiology as a cold and moist food, must be "corrected" with hot and dry flavorings. This is to prevent corruption, to which all phlegmatic foods are subject, including peaches and melons, but also to make it a humorally balanced or tempered food. The condiments in question would include pepper, cinnamon, and anything spicy, like mustard. The combination of pork and mustard may very well have an origin in medical theory. Cameline sauce is a ubiquitous medieval condiment, made by pounding cinnamon with raisins, walnuts, and bread with a little vinegar until it makes a smooth sauce. The name probably comes from *canella*, the old word for cinnamon. Some recipes include garlic as well.

try a piece. (You really shouldn't eat it, I guess. A good poke will do.) If it seems quite tough, then it is. Also, if the meat smells oddly metallic and has a sticky darkness to it, the animal was probably panicky when shot. Panicked meat loses its lactic acid stores, so try soaking such meat overnight in cultured milk—buttermilk, whey, yogurt. But in any case, don't expect bland domestic flavor when you taste wild meat.

My Grandma Nafziger uses braising to turn economy cuts into company fare. For her, that often meant elk, venison, or moose. She worked as a missionary in a part of Canada where mail didn't come in the winter. Try braising venison heart if you're curious about heaven. Economy or no, I'll always prefer falling-off-the-bone braised meat to the choicer cuts that get the steak treatment. I'm probably half made of braised venison.

Trim the fat from several pounds of meat and cut into similarly size pieces. Heat the trimmed fat, and, if necessary, some extra butter in a large, heavy skillet or Dutch oven. Put a single layer of meat in the bottom of the pan and let it brown, undisturbed, for a minute or two. When it comes away easily, flip the pieces and let them brown on the underside. Remove from the pan and brown the rest of the meat similarly.

Return all the meat to the pan. Add salt, pepper, a few bay leaves, a few diced onions, a chopped carrot, and a cup of water or wine. If you'd like more broth, use a deep dish and more liquid. Some root vegetables and a nice soup bone are quite pleasant, or a spoonful of honey. Bring to a boil, cover, and bake in the oven at 325 degrees for at least four hours. Add some crushed garlic toward the end of the cooking time.

To make gravy, bring the drippings to a simmer. Rub two tablespoons of flour into two tablespoons of butter. Add it to the simmering drippings and stir until smooth and thick.

—R

RENDERING FAT

In addition to being the very best way to season your cast-iron cookware, home-rendered fat is infinitely versatile and nutritious. Unlike supermarket lard, home-rendered lard hasn't been partially hydrogenated for stability, and is a rich source of essential fatty acids and vitamin D if it comes from healthy hogs. Bear fat, which most bear hunters have in excess, is a delicious light oil, liquid at room temperature. The fat of waterfowl like ducks and geese is extraordinary—for frying, roasting, or just for putting on toast. Chicken fat, the original *schmaltz*, is less exciting, but it certainly works.

Get at least a couple of pounds of fat from your desired animal. A good butcher should supply it to you inexpensively, since it's one of those wonderful things other people are afraid to mess with. Note that fat from different parts of the pig yields different grades of lard. The best is leaf lard from the kidney area, which is prized for pastry-making, but the other fats will do very well for frying. If you have a whole duck or goose on hand, be sure to scrape the fat from inside its cavity—it should yield quite a bit, which you should save for rendering.

Chop or grind the fat as finely as you can—this will make for a more efficient extraction, particularly important for pork fat. Put the fat in a large skillet, allowing for extra sizzle room, and cover with a cup or so of water per skillet. Set in the oven on the lowest setting, open a window, and let it slowly render overnight. Take care that the water doesn't all evaporate, or the fat will brown and gain a meaty flavor.

The bits of connective tissue that held the fat together will shrivel up and form cracklings as the fat renders. When they are emptied of their fat, they sink to the bottom of the pan. This is your sign that the fat is rendered. If at the end of rendering, there is still water under the fat, you can let it cook off, at risk of burning the fat. Or you can chill the fat until solid. Lift it out of the pan; any water that hasn't evaporated will remain in the bottom. Put the fat back on the heat and gently melt it. Pour it through several layers of cheesecloth to strain out the cracklings. Ladle it into jars and store it in a very cool room or the refrigerator. The cracklings are delicious.

Your skillets will be seasoned for life.

Of course, you should always save the informally rendered fat that rolls off when you roast a duck or fry bacon. That sort of fat is great for quick frying, but for deep frying, you really need the fat to be as pure as can be.

—R

Meatballs

If you are in a very serious mood, and girded with a capacious appetite, tackle the indomitable meatball. For many years, I was convinced that a meatball must be made with no less than three varieties of flesh (to wit: beef, pork, and veal), must be held together with bread soaked in milk, and must be gently sauteed in a pan. The flavor is somewhat superior when they are fried, but try plopping the raw balls directly into the gently simmering sauce; the texture is infinitely more pleasing. The meatballs actually soak up the sauce, and the juices of meat and tomato meld. Furthermore, stale old bread crumbs pounded in a mortar (one of my favorite things) can go directly in the mix, with Parmigiano and oregano, and (dare I say it?) ground turkey is just fine on its own. The nicest thing about these is you can let them cook on the barest simmer forever, and they remain unctuous and soft.

Start with a pound of ground beef, pork, turkey, or any combination of these. Add half a cup of grated Parmigiano; a cup of coarsely pounded bread crumbs; and herbs such as oregano, basil, and thyme. There is no need to add eggs, which will toughen up the mixture. Mix thoroughly and roll into balls any size you like. Drop these delicately into a pot of gently simmering tomato sauce. Don't stir, or the meatballs may fly asunder. After 10 minutes or so, they will have solidified, but feel free to simmer as long as you like; they will never overcook.

—K

Pork Pie

I believe it is always a good practice when trying something utterly new, to begin by following a recipe to the best of your ability, and thereafter never do so again. This was the case with a pork pie, for which to start I deferred to the wisdom of Jane Grigson, in *Good Things*, a Thoroughly British Book. And yes, the hat takes its name from the pie, not the other way around.

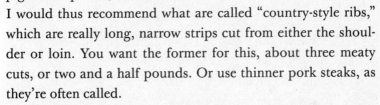

A beautiful lard-based crust atop a pork pie.

To begin with, get some pork shoulder; the fattier the better. Pig fat is the sort of thing few butchers keep around anymore, not only because pigs are leaner, but most of the pig comes precut, without much fat. I would thus recommend what are called "country-style ribs," which are really long, narrow strips cut from either the shoulder or loin. You want the former for this, about three meaty cuts, or two and a half pounds. Or use thinner pork steaks, as they're often called.

Remove the bones, chop the meat into small pieces, and either grind them finely or chop them as finely as you can with two cleavers. I like the coarse texture left by the latter, and the chance to wail on the cutting board. Season with fresh sage, ground cinnamon, cloves, nutmeg, and a tablespoon of salt. As with sausages, a pinch of instacure #1 (sodium nitrite) will keep the filling pink and lively tasting.

Next, there is a hot water crust, something as frightening as it is delicious. Mix four cups flour, a teaspoon of salt, and a tablespoon of powdered sugar in a bowl. Then take one cup each of water and lard and boil in a pan. Pour the boiling lard mixture directly into the flour and stir vigorously. Divide into two balls, one bigger than the other. Roll these out as quickly

A MEDIEVAL PORK PIE

A traditional, let's say Victorian-era, pie can be molded by deft hands free form around a wooden pie mold, or cylinder-shaped jar, and decorated with scraps of dough. But let's turn back the clock further. This basic filling was once much more interesting, the spice mixture being the only remnant of its glorious origins. First I would suggest dried fruit soaked in wine adds immeasurable depth and texture to the filling. Prunes, figs, or even apricots chopped into small pieces lend grace. But do not stop there. Ginger is perfect here; the dried powdered form is appropriate for the medieval era, plus a little more sugar. Candied citron peel is perfect. Then skip the jellied stock step and pour in some vinegar; verjuice, the juice of pressed unripe grapes, is even better. Lemon or sour orange juice also works and cuts through, conceptually, the idea of eating handfuls of lard. And if that part keeps you from trying this recipe, then let's go for complete authenticity. Think of the crust not as the lovely crunchy side to your slice of pie. Think of it as a container for dead meat—the "coffin," as it was called, made from flour and water; rye was said to hold up best. The purpose is merely to hold everything in hermetically sealed, but the thick crust is not eaten. Look at any pie in an early modern still-life painting: It's broken open and the contents scooped out and served. Why trust me here—follow the recipe for "Crustade gentyle." Here the crust is blind-baked, and unlike the Crustade Ryal, which precedes it, does not contain the riot of spices, sugar, raisins, and dates. Also, the author omits to mention baking, before service.

A RENAISSANCE PIE

Here is a variation using mutton or beef that offers a kind of short-crust pastry instead, from *A Proper Newe Booke of Cokerye*, the aesthetic very much 16th century. The powdered beef—we would call corned beef—and here the cooking liquid is used as the stock poured in at the end. It is not unrelated to the original mincemeat pie.

To Make Pyes

Pyes of mutton or beif must be fyne mynced and ceasoned wyth pepper and salte, and a lyttle saffron to coloure it, suet or marrow a good quantitie, a lyttle vyneger, prunes, greate raysins, and dates, take the fattest of the broathe of powdered beyfe, and yf you wyll have paest royall, take butter and yolkes of egges, and so tempre the flowre to make the paeste.

—K

as you can while still quite hot, putting the larger into the pan, the smaller set aside covered in plastic wrap for the top.

Firmly press the pork filling into the bottom crust, wet the edges of the dough, and put on the reserved top crust. Crimp by pressing the edges with the tines of a fork, or do whatever you have to, to keep the two halves together, and trim the edge. The dough tends to crack, very much unlike short butter pastry, so work quickly. Put a big hole in the top, and bake for two hours. Be sure to put a baking sheet under the pan, for it may very well bubble over a bit.

I will leave the next step to your discretion. You can make a stock from scrap bones and trotters with vegetables and a bouquet garni, boiled down to a thick jelly. It is gelatinous, and puts off an intense piggy odor. And pig feet are not easy to find. If you cannot abide by such antiquation, use a cup of good chicken stock, thickened with a (quarter-ounce) packet of gelatin. In the last 15 minutes of baking, brush the top with beaten egg. When the pie comes out, get a funnel, and *very slowly* pour in the gelatinous broth, spoonful by spoonful. This will slowly seep in and not only flavor the entire pie but keep it together when cool. It can be eaten warm, but improves when the gelatin is set.

—*K*

Rabbit

It's a shame that people are eating less rabbit nowadays. I know, they're cute and cuddly. Indeed they are, which is the very reason I will not have them as pets: I would either end up eating the pets one hungry day, or would never be able to cook rabbit again. Here is my insight on bunnies. They should not be thought of as vaguely like chicken. Yes, the flesh is light colored, and if you fry the legs, you might even fool someone. But commercially raised rabbit is too dry to cook like chicken. Hare or wild rabbit may be another matter, but farm-raised is what's commonly available. Nonetheless, the flavor of rabbit only comes through when it is stewed. Use some broth and onions, or even a light tomato sauce as a kind of *sugo*. Mushrooms are an ideal partner. Rabbit bones are a bother in the end, but it is well worth it. It takes the longest, slowest cooking you can manage, and I suggest a pot that is sealed tightly with dough, and therefore never opened or stirred.

My favorite way of making rabbit is "smeared" in a pipkin, which is a little three-legged vessel from Elizabethan times that sits over hot coals in the fireplace. A proper original recipe follows. One can use a regular oven as well. The secret is to use a clay vessel if possible, stuff it to the very top with ingredients, use very little liquid, and seal it with dough. Just flour and water works fine; you want it sturdy. You can, incidentally, also use a chicken, rammed into a pot that will just barely hold it, with mushrooms and sliced onions. It works almost as well. The trick is to cook it at 250 degrees for about five hours, or a little hotter if you don't have that much time, but not over 300 or it will burn. A porringer is a little drinking cup, about the size of a small teacup. The verjuice in the recipe is unripe grape juice; a little lemon will work in its place. The currants are tiny raisins, not the fresh fruit called currants. The *soppes* are thick slices of bread that soak up the juices when served. If you can't find barberries, no matter. Any tart berry would be nice.

How to smeare a Rabbet or a necke of Mutton (fol. A5)

Take a pipkin, a porenger of water, two or three spoone-
fuls of Vergis, ten Onions pilled, and if they be great quarter them, mingle as much the Pepper and salte as will season them, and rub it upon the meat, if it be a rabbit put a
piece of butter in the bellye and a peece in the broth, and
a few currans if you will, stop your pot close and seeth it
with a softe fier but no fier under the bottom, then when
it is sodden serve it in upon soppes & lay a few Barberies
upon the dish.

*The Good Hous-wives Treasurie. Beeing a verye necessarie Booke
instructing to the dressing of Meates*, printed in London in 1588.

RABBIT FRICASSEE

Another way to make rabbit is less exacting, but equally interesting in flavor. Simply cook a few slices of chopped bacon.
Remove the bits and brown the jointed and seasoned rabbit in
the remaining grease. Add an onion or shallots, some capers,
a few slices of lemon, and some sprigs of rosemary on top. Pour
in dry white wine to cover the rabbit. Put a lid on it and stew
slowly for about two hours, without stirring, but checking now
and then to make sure the liquid hasn't evaporated. Add more
wine if necessary. Toward the end you can add some chopped
tomato or even a dash of cream. Serve with small roasted
potatoes.

RABBIT PIE

Lean, dark rabbit meat is delicious drowned in gravy and baked between layers of flaky pastry. I asked my mother's mother for her very-German hunting-party pie. "Oh dear," she said, "we old Pennsylvania Dutch don't cook so much with recipes." I told her that was fine; I usually didn't, either. "Well," she said, "I cooked the rabbit and made a gravy with the broth. Then I made a rich pastry, put the meat in with some potatoes, carrots, and onions, poured the gravy over, and covered it up with pastry." Sealed under the crust with that magical gravy, the vegetables steam gently while soaking up the meaty flavors.

First, select a young rabbit, preferably less than three pounds. If necessary, clean and dress it and break it down into several large pieces. If you'd like, this recipe is just fine (but not more than "just fine") with chicken—even an old stewing hen if you subject her legs to a very long braise. Use just the dark meat, as breast meat doesn't hold up to the long cooking. Heat a little oil in a large pot over a medium-high flame. Salt the meat and add it to the pot, letting it brown without moving for a few minutes before you flip it and let it brown on the other side. When golden, add just enough water to cover the meat, top with a lid, and let it simmer while you make the pastry, chop the vegetables, till the garden, and hang out the laundry for nine children; that is to say, the longer it simmers, the better.

For the pastry, put three cups of flour in a bowl and sprinkle with salt. Grate in a quarter pound frozen lard, tossing the fat into the flour with a fork. Don't let the fat melt and blend with the flour—this is easy to do with lard, which is softer than butter. Sprinkle the mixture with two tablespoons water and toss to distribute the moisture. Repeat three to four times, until the dough is still quite crumbly but holds together when pressed. Push into a ball, cover with a plate, and chill while you work on the filling.

At this point, heat your oven to 425 degrees and remove the meat from the broth. It should be very tender. Put it on a plate to cool so you can pick it from the bone without burning yourself, and let the broth continue simmering. You want to end up with about two cups of broth. If it looks like you have significantly more, let it boil down uncovered while you chop the vegetables: two potatoes, two onions, and two carrots, all cut into medium-small dice.

Next, make the gravy. In a little skillet, melt four tablespoons butter over medium heat. Sprinkle on four tablespoons flour and stir gently until it turns just golden. Add to the reduced broth and stir until thickened. Taste the gravy. It needs salt and pepper in quantities sufficient to accommodate the vegetables, too, so season generously. Turn off the heat and let the gravy wait.

Lightly flour a rolling surface and place two-thirds of the dough on it. Press down with the rolling pin to mash it together and flatten it. Lift the dough and sprinkle flour beneath it, lightly flour its surface, and commence rolling it from the center outward into a 15-inch circle. Fold it in half and lift it carefully into a No. 9 cast-iron skillet. Unfold the dough, center it, and gently coax it into the corners and then up the sides. Trim the dough, leaving a one-inch overhang. Use the scraps to patch any holes, with a dab of water for glue. Set aside, clean the dough globs from your rolling surface, and roll the remaining dough into a 12-inch circle.

Pick the meat from the bones and place with the vegetables in the pie shell. Pour the gravy over. Dab the rim of the bottom crust with water, fold the top crust in half, and place it on top of the filling. Trim any excess to match the bottom crust and pinch the two together. Double the rim, folding the overhang back on top of the crust, and crimp the edge. Cut a few slits in the middle of the top crust, and put it in the oven.

Bake until the crust has started to color—about 15 minutes—then reduce the temperature to 350 degrees and continue baking until the gravy is bubbling in the middle, 45 minutes to an hour more. You may need to recut the slits partway through if they seal over in the oven.

When it's done, pull it from the oven and let cool for 10 minutes. The insides will need a chance to stop their bubbling and thicken up.

—R

Olla Podrida

Among our hodgepodge of meaty stews, the classic, using practically all the meats mentioned heretofore, must not be neglected. This is the Spanish *Olla Podrida*. These words in translation are enough to put you off; they mean *putrid* or *rotten pot*. But it is delicious when cooked right. In the *Arte de Cocina* by Martínez Montiño (1611), the author opines, "Take lamb, beef, bacon, pig's feet, testuz (nape), lucanega sausages, tongues, pigeons, duck, hare, beef tongue, garbanzo beans, garlic and turnips in season, and whatever meat you want, and mix it all in an olla, and let it cook long in the olla. Add your spices, and when it is well cooked, make plates of it." It's served with mustard and a sprinkle of parsley.

I like his spirit—throw in whatever you want. I would say the tongue is really what makes the dish, partly because you can imagine it tasting you back if you're really deranged. The chickpeas are also essential, and the sausages. But from there, chuck in anything. When you get to the later 17th century in cookbooks like Robert May's or Bartolomeo Stefani's, they throw in marrow, chestnuts, cockscombs (yes, the little red wiggly things are edible) and testicles, candied citron, musk, and ambergris. The latter is spewed up from whales' guts and after floating in the ocean takes on an ethereal perfume.

This procedure is a perfect hodgepodge and, when it comes out of the oven (I also like cooking it in a fire pit), it looks like a mess, but it tastes incredible.

—K

An Ode to Tongue

Did dulcet tones from these realms resound?
Once the Parnassus of bucolic bound
Whose MOOS inspired great poets to sing
Filled valley and pasture with sonorous spring
Yet now at the deli three blocks down the street
Lowered to the level of cheap luncheon meat
Artfully indolent this bovine before us
Dismembered of voice that once rose in chorus
So Irvings and Abes who cold cuts require
Now are heirs of the Orphean lyre
By eating imbued with lyrical knack
Or is the poor beast merely tasting them back?

—K

Smoking

There is something about the scent of wood smoke that triggers a primeval nerve center in the brain and signals pleasure and comfort. Any smoked food does the trick: meat, fish, or vegetables, even cheese. No doubt our prehistoric progenitors sitting around a fire learned to appreciate the flavor over the centuries and now the trait is hard-wired into the species. In fact, I am convinced that along with sweetness and salt, smoke is a basic primary flavor. Although smoking can serve as a preservative along with a cure, here it will be treated primarily as a flavoring agent. The process couldn't be simpler.

First you will need a smoker. There are excellent commercial smokers available that cost no more than a small barbecue grill. A little door at the bottom lets you tend to the smoldering embers. There is also a pan fitted beneath the rack so the heat is indirect; a small tinfoil packet of aromatics can be placed in the pan, with or without water. If you don't own a smoker, use a metal trash can with large holes poked in the lower half, a makeshift door, and a few nails hammered into the upper portion, on which you can lay a grill grate without it falling in. The ideal and traditional way to smoke is simply to build a small wooden shack. Meat is hung from the rafters and a small fire smolders in one corner.

There are two kinds of smoking: cold smoking and hot smoking. Apart from the temperature difference, only the latter really cooks the food through. Fish and vegetables can be cold smoked alone and certain types of cured meat. For the sake of flavor, rather than long storage, I have found it is best starting the smoke colder and then letting the flame build up toward the end. Either way, the process is the same to start. Begin by seasoning your food. Fish such as salmon or trout can be simply salted and seasoned with dill or tarragon and left overnight to cure. Meat can be given a dry rub and left to cure in the fridge anywhere from a few hours to a couple of days (see page 120 for more on curing). The dry rub can be a combination of salt, sage, paprika, thyme, mustard powder, pepper, whatever you like. The longer it is left to cure, the deeper the flavor.

Although you can smoke a whole turkey or leg of pork, smaller cuts of meat are easier to deal with, and will cook through to the center without the exterior becoming too dry and oversmoked. A turkey breast that has been flattened by breaking the breastbone, or a pork loin roast is ideal. The latter is basically two pork loin sections seasoned and tied together into a round roast. A pork shoulder also works fine. So, too, does a whole chicken with the backbone removed and flattened. Any light meat is fine, as are sausages.

Once the meat is well seasoned, start a regular campfire in the smoker. This means some crumbled newspaper, some twigs arranged in a teepee on top, and then some larger sticks. On top of this, place a single section of log; it is easiest to saw a log in half to fit in the smoker. Oak works fine, but apple or cherry are even better. Just don't use pine or the food takes on a strange resin-y flavor. Almond wood is really pleasant. If you can get mesquite or hickory wood, go for it. But don't use charcoal or briquettes—what you want is wood smoke, not intense heat. You can also use wood chips, but just remember the soaking they usually recommend is for use over direct heat, to create a steamy smoke on a regular grill. We are using much cooler, dry, and indirect heat, so there is no need to soak chips.

Light the fire and let it burn for about 10 minutes. Then put the food on the rack, into the smoker, and cover with the lid. Once you cover it, the flame goes out, but the block of wood smolders. The smoker allows in just enough air so the flame doesn't go out completely, but not enough for it to remain on fire. If you have a smokehouse, it is the same process: just a smoldering log in the corner and the meats hung from the rafters. Depending on how intense you want the smoky flavor, anywhere from an hour to two or three will be sufficient. The heat will be about 130 to 150 degrees or so in the smoker. This is technically hot smoking and will actually cook the food. If you are smoking fish, you want it below 100 degrees, and they'll be ready to serve anywhere from 45 minutes to an hour. With meat, you do want to cook the food through, so after a few hours at 130 to 150 degrees, open the door of the smoker and the rush of air will set the log on fire again. The heat will crank up, but since the flame is far from the food, it won't char as it would on a barbecue. About half an hour with the lid on and the door open will cook the meat through. You can serve it hot, or let it cool and slice for cold cuts, which are magnificent.

Just keep in mind that we are smoking here for flavor; long-term preservation is much trickier, so plan on eating the food smoked this way within a few days, and store in the fridge. You can make your own bacon, ham hocks, or smoked turkey legs following this method, but these are not cured for long storage, and of course will need to be cooked or tossed into another dish to cook. Think of a pot of lentils or beans, a soup, or slow-simmered greens.

—K

Pastrami: Seasoned, Smoked, and Steamed

The best pastrami in the universe is said to be found at Langer's in L.A. (New Yorkers, insert raspberry here.) Katz's in New York does hold a candle to it. But I made a pilgrimage to Langer's with my pals Andrew and Damon, and it was indeed stupendous, but not, it must be admitted, superior or even markedly distinguished from their equally fine corned beef. So in the spirit of homemade one-upmanship, I offer you these directions for a staggeringly toothsome pastrami, though it is not technically cured, as no nitrites are used.

The cut is traditionally the fatty beef belly, but if your butcher has no such thing on hand, a brisket will work just as well. Make a rub using two good handfuls of sea salt, a ton of pepper, and spices at your discretion. I prefer quite spicy, aromatic, and even resinous flavors, so I add in a good tablespoon each of cardamom, coriander, and juniper berries, and a hint of fennel. Rub these onto the meat until covered all over; you may not need it all. Wrap tightly in plastic or in a big Ziploc bag and place in a capacious metal roasting pan and place a board on top. Put in the fridge and load anything heavy on top of the board. Turn over every few days for a week to 10 days. **Note:** Since you are not using nitrates or nitrites, the flesh will not be red. So what? You're not storing this for months, so there is really no need to use them, at least for this recipe.

After the week or so is up, smoke the meat gently for about two hours in your smoking contraption, as noted previously. Then let it rest another day before steaming it, or if you are impatient, proceed immediately to the steaming. This must be a gentle affair, on a rack set over water in a large pot, for a good four hours if you can, to achieve unctuous succulence. Do not boil, as with corned beef, or you will dilute the lovely smokiness and exotic spicery. Slice thinly and put on toasted sourdough rye—your own from page 90, with lashings of brown mustard, perhaps horseradish if you must, or even, if you desire sandwich apotheosis, some of your own sauerkraut. And will we balk at some Swiss cheese, and frying the whole lot in a little butter for something Rubenesque? I say not!

—K

Beef Jerky

One can make extraordinary jerky using the exact same smoking method offered earlier. I was supplied by my next-door neighbor with a practically fat-free round roast from her father's ranch of grass-fed beef. Any very lean beef will work fine. Partially freeze, or defrost the meat so it can be sliced thinly, across the grain, into four- or five-inch strips. Season these with a dry rub. My older son, Ethan, invented one made with judicious quantities of salt, pepper, cumin, paprika, and oregano, with a hint of chili flakes. A small bowlful was enough to season a five-pound roast. But season just as you would any piece of meat: not too heavily. Then place on a metal grate in a single layer in the smoker. I used two racks of meat, one on top of the other, separated with three rocks so the air could circulate. About one hour is enough to give the meat an intense smoky flavor. Then put the rack in the oven at 150 degrees for a few more hours to make sure they're thoroughly dried. I have also done this with antelope, which was divine.

One can also very easily skip the smoking part entirely and just dry the strips slowly. There is absolutely nothing to it, just forget about it in the oven for 6 to 10 hours at 150 degrees, or even overnight, until the meat is thoroughly dehydrated. I made a batch with venison this way, which turned out spectacular. For variety, try adjusting the seasonings. Although the basic Mexican-type rub makes sense, you can also do a Middle Eastern rub with sumac, oregano or za'atar, and chili that is very interesting. Asian flavorings also go nicely: soy, ginger, a touch of brown sugar and garlic, but with a wet marinade, you will have to let the meat sit for a day or so and it will take longer to dry later, but it gives the meat an unctuous sheen. If you are truly adventurous, try to make pemmican, which is equal amounts of dried meat—venison is fine—pounded into a fine powder, then mixed with an equal part bear fat, and cranberries or other tart berry, and store in a leather pouch until needed.

—K

Ham: Smoked but Uncured

Here is a long and laborious method for making ham that will not preserve the meat for long keeping, but tastes so good that you will wonder why you ever bought mass-produced ham. It is not, I will readily admit, anything like the glorious prosciutto, serrano, or even Smithfield. It is not a dried ham. It is more like what they call in Britain bacon, especially since it comes from the same part. You can use any cut really, but for nice slices, a pork shoulder "butt," or what is sometimes called a picnic ham, is a perfectly pleasant size and won't set you back a fortune as will a whole leg. You can also use a tenderloin, which will give you a kind of Canadian bacon.

First tie up the pork, or buy it already tied as a roast. Mine was five and a half pounds. Make a brine with a pot of water; a handful of salt; a dash of vinegar; and spices such as cloves, coriander, and bay leaves. Add some sugar and molasses for color. Boil all this together in a stockpot for about an hour and then cool. Plop in the pork and let it sit for a week, completely submerged. You are basically corning the meat. This works nicely for beef, too. It's not very different from the brine you might use for turkey or chicken, but obviously it soaks longer. Note that in this case, you do need to put it in the fridge. Turn it over every day or so for five days or longer. Traditionally, saltpeter (potassium nitrite) would have been added to keep the meat pink, and you can use a pinch of sodium nitrate (instacure #1), if you like.

Remove the pork from the brine, and place it in your smoker. Slowly smoke for about three hours or longer, depending on how deeply flavored you want it. I also put in the smoker a little tinfoil packet of sea salt, opened at the top, which itself smokes. Poke the meat, and depending on the temperature in your smoker, it may still be soft. This means it is not cooked. You can either feed the fire with more wood to bring the temperature up to completely cook the pork, or put it in the oven at 350 degrees for 30-minute intervals, checking at the end of each, until meat is firm. You can test for internal temperature with a meat thermometer if you are a worrisome sort, which the government recommends at 160 degrees, at which point you will have shoe leather. I take it to 140, or simply poke and prod for doneness.

Let it cool, slice, and serve. Do not be alarmed; it will be fairly pink in the middle. That's what you want. If you overcook it, it will become tough and dry. The next morning, take a few slices of the ham and fry it in a cast-iron skillet in plenty of butter until nicely browned. Sprinkle with smoked sea salt if you like. In the South, they traditionally deglaze the pan with coffee or even cola. The meat gets crispy edges like good British rashers. Perfect with toast and fried eggs, sunny-side up, a side of baked beans, and a roasted tomato.

—K

Cured Meats

There is probably no topic treated by food writers with greater forewarning and trepidation than curing meats. One book I bought was downright arrogant, intoning essentially that "this is not a book for beginners and don't even try the recipes here unless you have had years of experience." Thanks, if I had years of experience, why would I need your book? How then is one supposed to get started? If you are a safe, play-by-the-rules type of person, do buy all the equipment and follow the detailed scientific instructions proffered by experts. If you care to try this as a beginner, read on. With a few basic precautions, there is no reason not to cure your own meat, nor quake in fear at the prospect of poisoning yourself. If you plan to cure a lot of meat or do it often, the equipment would make it easier. I don't have a single machine, only a simple plastic funnel.

Admittedly one does want to avoid botulism, whose very name in Latin derives from the word for sausage—*botulus*. Thus we turn to nitrates once again. One with a serious antiquated bent can try homemade saltpeter, which begins with a pile of manure, from which crystals are scraped. Saltpeter, potassium nitrate, is used by practically no one anymore, unless they're making gunpowder. It has almost completely given way to sodium nitrite, and there are specific formulae that also include sodium nitrate, intended to slow-release the right chemicals at the right stage in the cure.

What you want in this case is called instacure #2, slightly different from the one used for sausages. If you are interested, it is a pound of salt, an ounce of sodium nitrite (6.25 percent), and 0.64 ounces of sodium nitrate. But enough science; it's a pretty pink color and can be bought easily online. A pound costs $10 and cures 480 pounds of meat. The important ratio is a teaspoon per five pounds of meat.

Most recipes also tell you to use a commercial bacterial starter. This seems to me the equivalent of powdered instant yeast, and if you want to do this the old-fashioned way, you will have to depend on your own native lactobacilli, just as with sourdough bread. The biggest concern most modern authorities have is how to get the bacteria to colonize the chopped meat. Since you are using your hands, this should be no problem. This is the way it has always been done until a few decades ago.

LAMB SAUSAGES

While you can get away without pink salt for some smoked foods, sausages simply do not pass muster (or even mustard) without it. Pork is really the ideal sausage meat, but lamb also works well.

Take a fat shoulder lamb chop weighing about a pound, cut large hunks from the bone, and carefully snip the lean and fat into irregular, pencil eraser–size nubbins with a good scissor, or cut with a sharp knife. This is easier if the meat is semi-frozen. It should take maybe 10 minutes and what you want is clean, nicely separated bits, with no smear of the fat. To this add some oregano, maybe a good pinch of sumac, and a finely chopped clove of garlic. Then come salt, pepper, and just a tiny pinch of sodium nitrite (instacure #1), which you can buy online or in specialty stores. Mix it up and fill two generous-size sausage casings. If you have a stuffing machine, go ahead and use it. I use a funnel and my fingers. This can be tiresome if you are making a lot of sausages, but for a few it is no problem. You can also stuff sausage directly into the casings with your fingers, which is actually easier than using a funnel with a too-narrow aperture.

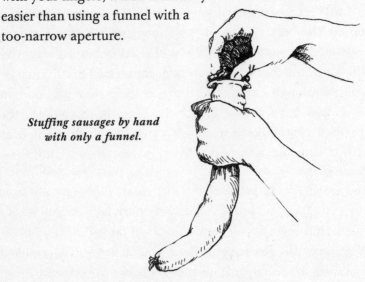

Stuffing sausages by hand
with only a funnel.

Put the sausages in the fridge for a few days. Then brown them gently in a cast-iron skillet in some olive oil. Serve on a heel of sourdough with good mustard. *Heavens!* They will be pink inside, with a delightful snap that makes me think of Nathan's hot dogs in Coney Island. Just salty enough, unctuous, and exactly what a sausage should be. It's all in the nitrite for flavor and all in the hand cutting for texture. After tasting these I actually tossed my cheap manual grinder in the trash—it makes a horrible mess of everything I've ever put through it. Nasty texture. From now on it's *fatto a mano*, literally.

Once you have the technique down, use pork shoulder or—as it is often called, "butt," which has just the right combination of fat (70 percent) and lean (30 percent). Add whatever flavorings you like: garlic, sage, and so forth. You can use pork casings, larger beef middles, or small sheep casings. Buy these online or from your butcher. You can also use veal for a *weisswurst*, but in that case you'll have to add some fat, ideally pork fatback. You can also pound the meat mixture in a big mortar if you want a finer texture, which works nicely for *weisswurst* or bratwurst. If you are adventuresome, you can also pound into a very fine paste for a kind of hot dog.

—*K*

SALAMI

For a classic salami, take five pounds of pork butt (shoulder) and a pound of fat. If you get a nice roast, you might not need any extra fat at all, but if you do, buy pork belly. If you want a rustic kind of look with visible hunks of fat, cut it all by hand. If you partially freeze it a little, it's much easier to cut. Take a few slices at a time and put the rest back in the freezer while you work, because if it gets to room temperature, it gets slippery and much harder to cut cleanly. Cut the whole thing, fat too, into neat little nubbins about the size of a pencil eraser top. Scissors work well for cutting up the meat cleanly and avoiding blisters.

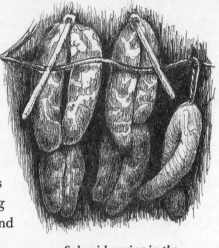

Salami hanging in the "cave" to cure and dry.

Here, the proportions of cure are very important. Add three and a half tablespoons of sea salt, four tablespoons of sugar—not to make it sweet, but necessary for the ferment—and a teaspoon of pink curing salt (instacure #2). The flavorings are up to you: I like oregano, pepper and a touch of a spice mixture I keep around made of cinnamon, cloves, nutmeg, cardamom, and ginger. Sort of like the French *quatre epices*. Just a pinch of mace would be fine, too. Garlic would be classic. Then add a quarter cup of red wine and mix it all well with your hands.

Now, if you really want to learn the meaning of the word *handmade*, get a funnel and push the opening of your casings onto the end, wetting them well first so they slide on. Push on about two feet's worth. I often use beef intestines or "middles"—which will leave your hands smelling like a bunghole for the rest of the day. You can soak them in water with a little vinegar to mitigate the odor. Pork casings are fine, too, but a little smaller. Tie the end of the casing off in a knot once it is on your funnel. With funnel in one hand, stuff mixture into the opening and gradually fill the whole casing. Remove sausage and tie off the other end. Twist it in the middle and tie with a string and you will have two-foot-long salamis. The five pounds of pork should make about 12 feet. Poke with a pin to let out air pockets.

Hang these in a cool place, around 55 degrees with a nice humidity—also necessary so they don't dry out too quickly on the outside, preventing the inside from drying evenly. A wine fridge works well for this. They should be ready in about four weeks. Even longer aging is fine if you want them to be harder. If you see flecks of white mold, that's perfectly fine. In fact, you can encourage it by buying a commercial dry salami and putting it in with yours. This adds to the flavor and helps preservation. These are what we would call *toothsome*. If you find the casing a little too chewy, feel free to peel it off. The fat inside the salami will be soft and yielding and balances beautifully with the firm, deep-red flesh. These will keep several months, becoming even drier and more complex in flavor. They can be stored at room temperature once quite hard.

For the sake of variety, you can mix half pork and half beef, throw in chili flakes and paprika, and a dash of vinegar instead of wine, for something like Spanish chorizo. Crushed fennel is also beautiful in salami. All beef ground finely with garlic will give you something more like a kosher salami. Keep in mind, you are making what you like—something uniquely yours, not trying to replicate some particular style.

If your salami smells bad or grows green mold, or if it seems unappetizing in any serious way, just throw it away and try again.

—*K*

7
Fish

Remarkably, fish are among the most expensive and elegant foods one can purchase; think of caviar, oysters, and lobster. They're also some of the cheapest; think of herring and squid. It all depends, of course, on the time and place. Near the Caspian Sea, any Russian could get his or her fair share of sturgeon eggs, and likewise stalwart Mainers glutted on lobster. Our coastal and riverine ancestors have always been great eaters of fish and seafood, as huge prehistoric shell middens attest. Preserved fish also provided winter provender, especially cod during Lent for Catholic countries. The ancient Romans prized fish above all other foods, especially giant mullet, for which they paid outrageous fortunes.

Today, one need not spend a fortune on good fish, but it is becoming increasingly difficult to find whole fish. Squeamish people have apparently prevailed at supermarkets, so nearly everything arrives in filets. This is a shame, not only because of the bones (necessary for stock), but because it is always good to know exactly where your food comes from. There is nothing like gazing deeply into a fish's eyes and taking a good whiff to determine its freshness. And then, there are fish that one can only find at the source, like the elusive abalone, which I have tasted exactly once in this lifetime while camping, when a diver literally handed me a monstrous white muscle after overhearing me talking about the impossibility of buying it fresh. It was pounded with a hammer and lightly fried, a revelation.

Whatever fish you can find and afford, preferably whole and smelling sweetly of the sea, treat it with care. Overcooking can quickly dry and toughen seafood, though a few of the antiquated recipes below prove notable exceptions to this rule.

Codfish

Cod, or *bacalao*, was not only historically important for meatless fasts throughout Europe, but it led intrepid 15th-century sailors all the way to Newfoundland to fish off the Grand Banks. The Norse still supply Italians and Portuguese with cod. The reason it has been so popular is that dried and salted cod lasts forever, and can be carried inland and left hanging through winter.

A distinction must be made between *bacalao*, which is salted codfish, and stockfish, which is cod merely dried without salt in the frigid air off the west coast of Norway, where it is called *tørfisk*. Stockfish must be pounded with a mallet before cooking, because it is as hard as a "stock" or log. *Bacalao* is merely soaked for 24 hours, changing the water a few times, or perhaps longer until no longer very salty. But it should not be oversoaked, or it loses much of its heady aroma.

BACCALÀ ALLA VICENTINA

Despite the name, this dish, from Vicenza, Italy, is traditionally made with stockfish, or *stoccafisso*, but you can also use salted *bacalao*. In either case, start with a stuffing of sauteed onions, garlic, and anchovies sprinkled with Parmigiano. Then roll a piece of stockfish fillet around a handful of filling, cover with milk and some olive oil, and slowly simmer for several hours. Sprinkle with parsley before serving. This is gorgeous served with polenta. And though it sounds fairly rustic, it is in fact as graceful and elegant as the Palladian mansions that dot the countryside.

BRANDADE

Bacalao makes a lovely *brandade de morue*, which is a smooth creamy dip from the South of France. Nowadays, people put potatoes in it for a really smooth texture. They use a food processor, too. Blech. You want the lovely stringiness from the fish that only comes from pounding in a mortar and pestle.

First poach the soaked and drained *bacalao* for about five minutes. Let it cool a little. Then break up a piece about the size of your hand, into your mortar. Start pounding, adding a clove of garlic. Slowly dribble in the best olive oil you can find. Fruity Ligurian is good, Niçoise even better, since the dish come from nearby Nimes. Use a good half cup of oil or more. Then add heavy cream, maybe a quarter cup. It is essentially a kind of mayonnaise without eggs. Season with pepper, thyme, or other herbs. It should be light and fluffy and delicate. You can even brown the top under the broiler in a gratin dish if you like. Serve with crusty bread.

CODFISH FRITTERS

Surprisingly, salted *bacalao* shows up as codfish fritters in Caribbean and west African cuisine, where you would think they had enough local fresh fish. In the Caribbean, dried codfish provided protein in the slave diet and persists among descendants of these very people.

Soak and poach the cod as above. Cool and flake finely. Mix with an egg, bread crumbs (but not too much), a good wallop of chili flakes, plus the tiniest hint of cumin, and even cinnamon. Roll into little balls and then roll these lightly in the crumbs. They can also be made into little patties, which are easier to cook. Fry in a pan in about half an inch of oil. Drain on paper towels and serve.

You can also use crab for this, and call them either crab cakes or croquettes if you're feeling fancy. If you're out of egg, a dollop of mayo works fine as binding. You can also throw in some chopped red onion, sweet bell pepper, or capers on a whim. I prefer no sauce if thus abetted, but if you must, a rémoulade works nicely or plain old tartar sauce. Both are basically just mayonnaise (see page 36) to which chopped capers, pickles, and herbs like parsley, chives, and tarragon are added. Add cayenne and it moves a little closer to Louisiana, likewise with Tabasco and horseradish. All these flavors go beautifully with *bacalao* or crab.

Another way to make these, and more typical in the Caribbean, is with a batter based on flour rather than crumbs, but in this case you will need to deep-fry them. You can also substitute conch for the ideal fish fritter.

—K

Tuna

We won't be talking about flaccid white flesh tuna from a can here; that goes best on white bread with mayonnaise. Think of the ancient tuna hunt off southern Italy, the *matanza*, in which tuna are corralled, gaffed, and lifted on board small boats. Such tuna is treated as flesh, not chicken of the sea, but in the past referred to by physicians as "beef of the sea."

TUNA STEAK IN RAMEKINS

Choose a deep-flavored meaty fish steak. Contrary to expectation, it can cook a relatively long time without drying out. Incidentally, this can also be made with the hunks of *bacalao* (mentioned earlier), or any firm-fleshed fish.

First, cut a piece of tuna from a large steak that will just fit inside a ceramic ramekin. Oil the ramekin well, then season the fish with sea salt, pepper, thyme, and perhaps a sprig of rosemary, finely chopped. Add some capers, a sliver of garlic, and a few raisins and pine nuts. Take a thick slice of the ripest tomato you can find, and place it on top. Drizzle it all with olive oil and pour in a splash of marsala or sherry, and bake in the oven for 30 to 40 minutes.

—K

TUNA SUSHI, TARTARE, OR CARPACCIO

It is really a shame to cook the finest sushi-grade tuna, so I exhort you to eat it raw in one of three ways:

1. Cut it into rectangular slabs. Period. Dip this for a second into *shoyu* (the original soy sauce) and pop whole into your mouth. Resist the urge to add wasabi, which overwhelms superb tuna. Equally, this needs no bed of rice. You can also cut it into smaller strips for a lovely poke salad as they do in Hawaii, garnished with seaweed.

2. The original tartare is named for the Tartars, who ate raw horsemeat. While horse as well as beef tartare have waned in popularity, tuna seems to be holding steady ground. Grinding ruins the texture, so I suggest chopping very fine. Create a mound with an indentation on top and drop in a raw egg yolk. Sprinkle with coarse sea salt. Nothing more.

3. Lastly, the upstart newcomer carpaccio, named after the Italian painter who loved bloody red colors. Cut translucent slices of tuna and lay them on a white plate. Drizzle with the best olive oil, a few drops of lemon, and coarse salt. A little watercress on top is lovely, too.

—K

Fish Stock

There is a great and understandable temptation to resort to a can when making soups. I don't mean completely premade soups, heaven forfend, I mean chicken or beef broth as a soup base. Some of them are quite good now, with reduced salt, especially

FISH IN THE UMU

This is a technique drawn from Polynesian cultures, and is found from New Zealand among the Maori straight across the Pacific to Hawaii. It is a cousin of the clam bake as well. Most often it is used for pork and starchy root vegetables like taro, which steam in a kind of underground oven. Fish cooked this way is sublime. It is especially good while camping because you literally need no utensils, pots, or anything. First dig a pit at least three feet deep; the width depends entirely on how many people you will feed. There is no reason not to do it for a small group. Make a fire in the pit and let it burn for at least an hour until the flames subside, and then throw some rocks on top.

On this you will put your package or packages of food. I like a mixture of shellfish and firm white fish. Take shrimp,

the organic ones that come in a carton. Even the concentrates are okay in a pinch. (I won't even mention the abomination known as the bouillon cube.) But there is really no reason not to make soup from scratch if you want to spend some leisurely time in the kitchen. A basic stock makes itself. A decent vegetable or fish stock can be made in half an hour, a good chicken stock in an hour or two. Beef does need some roast bones and then many hours to boil with carrots, onions, and celery. But once a stock is made, you can boil it down to a concentrate and freeze in cubes if you are so inclined. The difference in flavor is really worth the time, and can be used as the base for innumerable soups.

scallops, perhaps clams, and something like orange roughy, and add lime juice, chopped Thai chilies, roughly chopped shallot, salt and pepper, even a dash of fish sauce is nice. Take all the seasoned fish and place it on two or three big banana leaves. These can be bought at a good Asian grocery, usually frozen. Wrap the fish up tightly into a parcel and tie with string. You can make a few small packages this way, or one big one, which is a little more difficult to handle. Some people put the big parcel in chicken wire so it doesn't fall apart or fall in the fire, but a few smaller packages are easier to work with. You can also make one package of potatoes. Fill the stone-lined pit with the packages, put another few banana leaves on top, then cover the whole thing with dirt. Forget about it for about three hours. Then dig it up and eat it.

—K

The basic principle is nothing to fret over. You are just boiling the ingredients until all the flavor is gone, and then straining out the solids, using a big "China hat" cone-shaped strainer, a sieve, or even a fine-meshed colander.

For fish you'll need the head, bones, and tail. Ideally you'd filet a whole fish and keep these parts for stock. Or have your fishmonger save these parts for you. This may be difficult nowadays, as most supermarkets have filets delivered and never see a whole fish. But if you can get it, it is well worth it. Put the bones in a stockpot, cover with water, and add chopped vegetables and a complementary herb. Tarragon works nicely. Or you can make a bouquet garni with bay leaf, thyme, and parsley tied into a bundle. Or just throw them in. Bring to a boil, then lower at a simmer for about half an hour, skimming the foam that rises to the top every now and then, then strain. Voilà. If you want a clear soup, don't press on the solids. You can also throw in shrimp shells; a splash of wine also does wonders. After it is strained, add salt to taste, but not too much. You can always add more later. This is especially important if you're going to reduce it to make a sauce, in which case it would probably be too salty.

Basic Fish Soup

With this fish stock, you can make a soup out of just about any kind of light-textured fish that won't fall apart with cooking, plus shellfish. I like to use cod, halibut, or snapper, cut into chunks, thin slices of leek or onion, a finely cubed potato, and then a few other types of shellfish, such as scallops sliced horizontally, some crabmeat, or chopped clams. If you are so inclined, a dash of milk or cream will give you a good, honest chowder. I am, however, partial to what many consider heretical: Manhattan clam chowder, which uses tomato, chopped bell pepper, and onion. This base can also be used for a San Francisco cioppino, a Tuscan *cacciucco*, or even a simple kind of bouillabaisse. These are all classic fish soups, but trying to replicate them precisely without the exact species caught fresh in Livorno or Marseilles seems silly. Just remember, there are no rules. As long as you don't use an oily fish like mackerel, or something very delicate like flounder, you should be fine. The trick is to merely place the fish into the stock very gently after the vegetables are softened, and resist stirring violently, so they stay whole when served.

—K

Snails

Neither fish nor fowl, snails are among the poorest and most neglected but most delicious of little slimy critters. As mollusks, they are vaguely close kin to most of the shelled seafood we eat, and so we have included them here with other ocean-dwellers.

Please don't make the same egregious mistake I did when harvesting snails directly from the garden. If you take them all, they never come back. The tribe disappears. I suspect that one stray survivor may have warned the whole neighborhood, because even a few years later, I rarely see snails, though my neighbors insist they have them. On the first and fateful gathering I had about 50 fat succulent babies. Never using chemical fertilizers or pesticides, I was certain that they were okay to eat, though what a diet of boxwood might do, I couldn't say. If you are among those miscreants who think poisoning them is the only solution, consider eating them instead. The common garden snail, *Helix aspersa*, is the same one they gobble down in France, intentionally imported to California in the 1850s as a delicacy and since accidentally escaped as a garden pest. All land snails are edible though; these just happen to be the best.

For all snails, a good week's worth of purging is always a good idea. The purge is simple: Put them in a bucket, feed only once with oatmeal or cornmeal, a handful or so and keep the lid on firmly, or they will run away—but be sure to poke holes in the lid. They do need air. Disabuse yourself of the implacable notion that snails are slow. They sure can haul house. After a week or so, you will see the contents of their digestive tracts purged. Consider going a day or two without giving them food, or they'll taste a bit like meal, though some consider this cruel and stressful on the snail. If none of this appeals to you, or if you can't stalk them yourself, by all means use canned snails.

For cooking, we follow the advice of the exalted Auguste Escoffier, greatest of French celebrity chefs of the early 20th century, who suggests washing them in clear cold water, then blanching them in boiling water for five or six minutes. You get a sticky mucus in the pot, which should be skimmed and discarded. Keep boiling until the water is clear. Then remove them from the shells and trim off dark parts. He recommends cooking them, replaced in shells, in a wine-and-water mixture on a bed of carrots, onions, and shallots for three hours. You may want to wash them again after blanching, in many changes of fresh water, to remove the slimy mucus.

You can also take a more classic approach: Mix the boiled and shelled snails with butter, garlic, and parsley, return them to the shell (after boiling), and then bake them through about 20 minutes.

Snails are also wondrous in cooked dishes if you forget about the shells entirely. They meld beautifully with tomato sauce, for instance, and if you think of them gastronomically as a cross between a mushroom and shellfish, the possibilities are endless. Red wine and shallots go perfectly. I also insist that you try them in Paella (page 69) with rabbit.

—K

8
Poultry

Who would have guessed that a Southeast Asian jungle fowl could rise to become the most popular of modern sources of protein, or the Meso-American turkey right behind it? In fact, the huge popularity of chicken is quite recent, and mostly due to the ease with which we can raise the birds on an industrial scale. Normally chicken has been reserved for special occasions. As the old saying goes, if there's chicken on the table, it means someone's sick—the chicken or the person. But there are excellent antiquated recipes using chicken, not to mention a bevy of endearing wildfowl. Our main concern with the domesticated bird, though, is how much it has changed in the past century. No longer the barnyard-scratching, ornery old bird that took hours to stew and yielded genuine flavor, our poultry caters to infantile taste buds that prefer white blandness and dry, unpalatable, skinless chicken breast. So if you can, for these recipes seek out a truly free-range stewing hen, or even a good old-fashioned capon— as old as you can find—and you will come closer to tasting what our forebears enjoyed.

Chicken Stock

Chicken stock is ridiculously easy and simple. And don't deceive yourself—store-bought broth is mostly water and chicken flavor. It has none of the silky, substantive gelatin of good, slow-brewed stock, and won't cure anybody's flu.

Put several pounds of meaty bones (raw or leftover from some other use) in a large pot. Cover with plenty of water and start the pot toward a boil. While it heats up, add an onion (cut in half, peeled or not), a carrot, and a stalk of celery. When the liquid gets to an almost-simmer, turn the heat down about as far as it will go, cover the pot, and let the bones steep for hours upon hours. Overnight is fine; 24 hours, fine, but probably no more. Simmering or boiling will make for a cloudy stock.

When the stock is ready, strain it through a colander into another large pot. If you want to make a concise little reduction, boil down the stock—lid off, of course—until you have only as much stock as the unoccupied space in your freezer. Meanwhile, pick the good meat from the bones and use it for soups or curries or chicken salad.

Let the reduced stock cool a bit, then pour it into ice cube trays or other small containers, and freeze to use at your leisure. Remember that it's quite concentrated—add a frozen cube of stock to a cup of water and you'll have a nice, thick broth on your hands. Otherwise, just use the stock as is for soups, sauces, and savory choux paste. Or any of the other gazillion things that really aren't the same without good stock.

About salt in stock: Since you don't know how concentrated the stock will be when you go to use it, wait till you're tasting the end product to add any seasonings.

—R

Roast Fowl with Gravy

Thanks largely to Thanksgiving and the other winter holidays, roasting whole birds is a fairly common technique in the modern cook's repertoire. Sadly, most modern cooks start with inferior birds, and wind up facing a terrible dilemma: Should they overcook the breast and let it get dry, or undercook the legs and wings? I have always hated the dry white meat—and since I can usually find some fat-phobe who pretends to prefer the dry stuff, it hasn't been such a dilemma for me. In fact, it really shouldn't be so hard. Old-fashioned birds that peck around in the grass have delicious, rich, moist, dark meat all over. This meat is dark and rich because it's full of healthy omega-3 fats and the birds get a little sunshine and exercise—not because of some fancy baking technique involving reams of aluminum foil. In contrast, modern factory–farmed birds have such huge expanses of breast meat that they threaten to topple over whenever they try to move. No wonder they are pallid and dull—and not fit for human consumption.

For a really festive delight, go for the waterfowl. The thick layers of fat that keep geese and ducks from getting cold in the water also keep their meat moist and tender while roasting. When you are done, you'll have a bonus jarful of delicious fat for cooking.

These are basic directions for roasting a bird. All kinds of variations and additions are fun to try. For instance, basting with honey-butter and herbs near the end of cooking time will give you a delicious skin. Stuffing is always magnificent—try bread cubes mixed with salt, pepper, fresh sage and thyme,

BRINING

If you're at all afraid of your bird being dry, you're well advised to brine it. Brined meat is significantly moister than otherwise. Through diffusion and osmosis, brined meat draws in the salt and brine liquid. Salt also causes the meat proteins to coagulate and hold in the moisture when roasted.

The brine should be quite strong—about a cup of salt per gallon of water. To brine a large bird (say, a 15-pound turkey), you'll need a couple of gallons of brine.

First, make the brine: Bring to a boil a quarter of the total water you'll need. Add salt and an assortment of other seasonings as you see fit: perhaps a small palmful of peppercorns, juniper berries, allspice berries, or herbs. Maybe some sugar if you like (no more than half as much as the quantity of salt you added), or booze or chili peppers. Turn off the heat and let the mixture cool to room temperature. Add the remaining amount of (very cold) water, put it in a large stainless-steel pot, and submerge the bird (minus all the giblets) in the brine as best you can. If the whole bird doesn't stay under, you may need to rotate it eight hours through. Let it brine for up to 24 hours. Rinse the bird and pat it dry before roasting.

butter, and a little egg (and oysters, please!). A stuffed bird takes much longer to roast through.

Before your roast the bird, take all the giblets out and cut off the neck and feet (if it hasn't been done for you). Save the liver for other purposes, but put the heart, gizzard, neck, and feet into a saucepan, cover them with water, and bring them to a simmer. This will be your stock for making gravy.

Ready your roasting equipment (see Roasting, page 94), or preheat your oven to 450 degrees. Scrape the bird's cavity and rinse it well. Let it dry for a bit, then rub it all over with salt if it hasn't been already brined. If you're doing a turkey or chicken or other land bird, you should also rub it quite well with olive oil or butter. If you are using the oven, you can place the bird breast-side down on a roasting pan, in a large skillet on a bed of chopped onions, on a rack set in a sheet tray, or on anything, really, that's large enough to collect all the drippings and will keep the bird up above the bottom of the pan so it doesn't burn. You can truss the legs to help the bird keep its shape, but it will take longer and cook less evenly. Let the bird go for 20 minutes or so, then reduce the heat to 325 degrees, and baste it.

To baste, just spoon up the fatty drippings if you have a duck or goose, or use a spoon to rub oil, butter, lard, or some other delicious fat over a land bird. If you aren't using a spit, rotate the bird breast-side up halfway through roasting.

The size of your bird and the roasting method will determine how long it takes. Generally, 15 minutes per pound in the oven will give you a decent estimate, but the only way to know for sure is to stick a knife into the thickest part of the leg all the way to the bone. When the juices run clear, the bird is done.

Let the bird rest for at least 15 minutes while you make the gravy.

GRAVY

Pour the drippings from the roasting pan into a glass measuring cup. The fat will rise to the top after a few minutes. If you have roasted a duck or goose, most of the drippings will be fat, and you will have far more than you need for gravy. But any liquid that settles to the bottom will be delicious, as will the magnificent browned scrapings that collect all over the roasting pan.

Strain the stock from the neck bones and giblets, and pick the meat from the bones. Return the neck meat and the giblets to the stock. Add any liquid juice from the drippings and all the good scrapings from the roasting pan, and set aside. Put several spoonfuls of fat from the roasting pan into a large skillet and heat over a medium flame. Add several spoonfuls of flour—about a tablespoon per cup of stock—and stir around until evenly combined and lightly browned. Pour in the stock and stir until it comes to a simmer, thickens, and combines to form a smooth gravy. Season to taste with salt, pepper, and fresh herbs such as sage and thyme. Keep warm until served.

—R

Stuffed Conceited Chicken

The idea behind this recipe is very much like the "conceits" or tricks of which medieval and Renaissance cooks were fond. It surprises first because a chicken with four wings comes out, and then you proceed to slice directly through it. Start with two small chickens. Cut off the wings then remove the skin in one large piece; you can slice it down one end and pull it off, the only tricky part is pulling out the legs. If it tears a bit, don't worry. Do the next bird the same way, and place both skins side by side on a baking pan. Next, remove all the meat from the bones. Keep the breasts whole and the dark meat any way you can. Season the meat with salt, pepper, thyme, paprika, or whatever you like. Place two breasts on the skins, some dark meat on top, then the other two breasts to create a nice high pile of meat. If you have a sense of humor, add a few hard-boiled eggs inside the pile as well. Add some fat from the chicken cavity if you have it. Then fold over the skin and tie it up with string, approximating as closely as you can a chicken shape. Add all four wings to the sides, just tucked under, and set aside.

The neatest thing about this dish is it lets you have both roast chicken and a nice stock at the same time. Take all the bones plus onions, carrots, celery, bay leaf, and boil to make a stock. Reduce, season with salt, a dash of white wine, and add a little flour or starch if you want it thicker. This is the gravy.

The last hour the stock is reducing, roast the chickens in an oven at 400 degrees. Serve with the gravy on the side. Slice directly through the entire bird package, ideally getting a round of egg in the middle. The meat stays nice and moist, having been wrapped up tightly.

—K

Chicken Rollatini

This recipe falls somewhere between a chicken kiev, a saltimbocca, veal birds, and who knows what other classic recipes. Versions go back as far as the 16th century, and offer the option of using veal or turkey, a recent import from the New World.

It is an ideal way to deal with a meat that might otherwise be dull and dry. The rolls can be reheated, even served cold on a picnic, and are actually quite elegant served two on a plate. They require no sauce, since there is so much in the filling, but do accompany with a green vegetable, perhaps sauteed spinach and a rice pilaf.

Start with skinless chicken breasts. Slice them horizontally into two thinner cutlets and pound them between two sheets of plastic with a flat *batticarne* or other meat pounder that won't tear the flesh. Marinate these for a few hours in a combination of olive oil, white wine vinegar, garlic, salt, pepper, thyme, or some other herb. Then press the cutlets directly into coarse bread crumbs, pounded from a stale rustic loaf, crusts and all for good texture and crunch, mixed with some grated Parmigiano. On top of each lay a single slice of prosciutto (no need to use the best expensive imported stuff). On top of that lay a slice of Gruyère or decent Swiss cheese. You can also add a single sage leaf if you like. Roll these up tightly and secure with a toothpick. Then bake them at 350 degrees for about 40 minutes. The chicken will remain moist and the exterior crunchy and dripping with melted cheese.

Duck or Goose Confit

In a fridge-containing kitchen near a well-stocked butcher shop, it doesn't usually make very much sense to preserve meat. However, the artistry of preservation often improves the character of the meat itself—plus you can display your shiny jars of provender on a pantry shelf, instead of stuffing them in the back of a crowded refrigerator. Kitchen aesthetics are a very important source of inspiration, and glass jars full of food are very encouraging company.

Confit is simply meat preserved in fat. If you're working with whole waterfowl like ducks or geese, you will have plenty of fat to cure the legs. Less fatty animals, or legs by themselves, will have to borrow fat from elsewhere. I describe the process for two bird legs, but you can adapt the methods to other creatures or body parts or quantities quite easily. The legs of birds being a good deal cheaper than their breasts, I use those.

First, salt and season the legs. Mix together several tablespoons of good sea salt, some grindings of pepper, the leaves from a few sprigs of thyme, a crumbled chili pepper. Add some mashed garlic or shallot, or whatever you like to eat with birds— a pinch of sugar? juniper berries? Rub this mixture all over the legs. Pack the legs in a bowl, cover securely, and refrigerate for two days.

Unwrap the legs and put them in a skillet or casserole dish that holds them tightly, so a minimum of melted fat is needed to cover them. Preheat the oven to 300 and add enough rendered fat to barely cover the legs. This fat can be duck fat, goose fat, or lard. (See Rendering Fat, page 100.) Let the legs sputter and sizzle for several hours—you're trying to cook out all the moisture, so that the finished dish contains nothing but fat and meat. Moisture leads to spoilage.

When the meat is quite tender, pack the whole legs tightly in a jar and cover with the fat. Let it cool, and cap the jar. It will keep for several months in a cool pantry, which you can now honestly call your "larder."

To serve duck confit, pull the legs out of the fat and crisp them up in a hot oven. Or try shredding it, as below.

—R

QUAIL

These are one of the few birds, although domestically raised, which still taste wild and gamey. Maybe it's the diminutive size, the fact that they must be slightly undercooked, or the fact that a few whole tiny birds makes a nice starter. If you hunt, by all means do use wild ones. They are delicious split in half and grilled, and can stand up to just about any barbecue sauce. A Korean sauce heavy with chilies, garlic, soy, and sesame oil is beautiful. But here's an antiquated recipe that is fascinating and delicious. It comes from the greatest cookbook ever written, the *Opera* by Bartolomeo Scappi, chef to Pope Pius V in the mid-16th century. Like most of his recipes, Scappi offers several options, and here he is talking about roasting turtle doves or quail, and he offers this as variations. Fennel pollen, recently very trendy, was a common ingredient, and can be bought at Italian gourmet shops, or shaken from the

CONFIT SHREDS

If you have made your own duck confit (*confit du canard*) or have found a good supplier (as I have in local Grimaud Farms here in Stockton, California), let me tempt you to venture the following procedure. Even though the duck legs are already cooked, place them in a cast-iron skillet with a little olive oil, and some thyme, and let them brown very slowly, turning gently. Let them continue to cook on the lowest possible heat, uncovered, until they begin to fall apart. Pull the strands of flower heads of a fennel plant. It's the yellow powder and tastes just like fennel. The adobo is a sweet-and-sour mixture of vinegar; grape-must syrup or sugar; and spices like cloves, fennel, cinnamon, pepper, and garlic.

In this same way you can roast a quail when fat, the season for which begins mid August and last through all October. Though sometimes around Rome, and especially at Ostia and Porto, great numbers appear in the spring, nonetheless they're not such a good thing as when in season. Sometimes fat quail are cured with salt and fennel pollen, and left in a wooden or ceramic vessel for three or four days, and then fried in rendered lard with little onions and served hot sprinkled with pepper, or split them in half and let them marinate for a day in adobo, and then flour them and fry in rendered lard, and serve hot with sugar and orange juice over, or with the same marinade on top, hot.

meat apart with two forks and continue to cook until the bones can literally just be lifted out clean. You will have a very finely shredded pile of crisp duck meat, which is called *sfilati* in Italian. They also do this with horse meat in Manuta, which is another kind of confit, spicy and unctuous.

Back to the confit. This shredded duck is about as good as any food gets. Put it on pizza. Fill a taco. Add it to some simmering greens with a little extra duck fat. Best of all, put it in with a slow-simmering pot of beans. Amazing stuff.

—K

Chicken, Goose, or Duck Pâté

Here's the thing with pâté. It's going to be rich and muddy, because it's butter and liver. Some people put expensive liquor in it to brighten the flavors. Unfortunately, I only make a habit of stocking one type of liquor, and that is bourbon, and mostly I use it in truffles. A little bourbon and apple cider vinegar are perfect in pâté. As for the seasonings, I vary them according to season and mood. I'll do *cinnamon-cloviness* in the winter and garlicky-herby stuff in the summer, when I might even sub a little olive oil for some of the butter.

And for impressing surprise dinner guests—the ones who thought they could get the better of your hospitality by ambushing you—remember that a perfectly smooth soft pâté can be made with just a fork, provided you mince the onions and garlic well, and mash the livers with the fork in advance of beating in the butter. I've whipped it up for an appetizer with dozens of people breathing down my neck!

Fill a large pot halfway with water. Add a couple of leafy stalks of washed celery, a lot of sea salt, and some herbs and spices: bay leaves, peppercorns, allspice berries, juniper berries, a clove. Bring it to a boil and simmer for 10 minutes to steep the herbs.

Add one pound of chicken, duck, or goose livers and simmer for another 8 to 10 minutes; the livers should still be pink inside. Drain the livers and remove the spices and celery. Put the livers in a large bowl with half a pound of butter, a quarter of an onion (diced), three cloves of mashed garlic, two teaspoons of dry mustard, a grating of nutmeg, a pinch of spicy ground dried chili, a splash of apple cider vinegar, and a splash of bourbon.

Beat it well with a strong fork, or crank it through a food mill. When it's all quite smooth, taste it and add the appropriate amount of salt, knowing that if you use coarse sea salt, it will inevitably take a bit for the saltiness to infuse the whole pâté. You can put it in a shapely buttered dish and unmold it when it's chilled, or just put it in little crocks and scoop it out.

—R

9
Dairy Products and Cheese

The curious irony of dairy products, apart from human milk in infancy, is that they are a relatively recent introduction to the human diet, and are largely restricted to peoples of northern Europe and the Middle East—where they originated with the domestication of cattle. Drinking fresh milk is the real oddity historically, and few peoples have evolved to be able to digest it efficiently in adulthood. But bacterial fermentation has been the practical way to store highly perishable milk for at least the past ten thousand years. The bacterial fermentation also made it more easily digested.

The beauty of all dairy products is that they do taste of whatever the animals have been eating—fresh spring grass, hay, or industrial fodder and silage. Pasteurization robs milk of most of its flavor, and it is a shame that what we have gained in supposed safety, necessary now that cows are raised in huge factories, we have lost in unique flavor. If you have a chance to taste a fresh unpasteurized cheese direct from a farmer in Europe, perhaps a chèvre in France or a real mozzarella in Italy, I promise you will be overwhelmed. Here we offer some homemade approaches to dairy, the old-fashioned way.

Cultured Butter

The average grocery store only tells you half the butter story. Their standard butter, made from uncultured ("sweet") cream, either salted or not, is but a sad cousin to butter churned from cultured cream. Uncultured cream is plain cream that has been pasteurized to kill the bacteria naturally present in milk (and all living things). Most cultured cream has also been pasteurized, but has particular bacteria reintroduced in a process much like making yogurt. Incidentally, fresh unpasteurized milk from healthy cows is brimming with wholesome bacteria quite similar to the bacteria that get reintroduced in the culturing process.

The beauty of it is that cultured butter simply, miraculously, tastes more *buttery* than sweet butter—not at all tangy or cheesy or yogurty—but pure, fall-on-your-knees *buttery*. Since cultured butter has a lower water content than uncultured butter, not only is it the tastiest thing you could ever spread on your toast, but it's perfect for making flaky pastries, too. And it's ridiculously easy to make at home—easier than making sweet butter, in fact. Leave that potted fern on top of your grandmother's heirloom butter churn—all you need is a broad wooden spoon and a bowl.

Look for good, raw or non-ultra-pasteurized cream in a natural food store or the farmers' market, or talk to local dairy farmers (see Resources for raw milk sources). Steer clear of the "ultra-pasteurized" cream widely available in grocery stores, as its flavors have been thoroughly cooked out. If you want your butter to have a gorgeous golden hue, look for cream from grass-fed cows, as their milk has a greater vitamin A content. Get a couple of quarts of cream, at least.

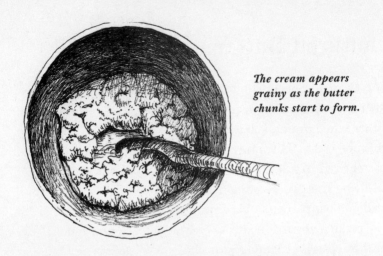

The cream appears grainy as the butter chunks start to form.

First, put your cream into a very large bowl. Add a good dollop of plain live-culture yogurt, mix well, cover with a plate or board, and let it sit in a warm spot overnight.

In the morning, stir the cream vigorously for a few minutes. It will start to thicken and look grainy. Keep stirring. Suddenly the butter clumps will stick together, and with a few more strokes, you'll have a lump of butter in a pool of thin, translucent buttermilk. Drain the buttermilk—but do save it for biscuits, or drinking straight!

Next, flatten the butter lump and chill it for a while, because it's still soft and warm from being left out overnight. When it's stiffer, take

Knead the butter thoroughly under running water.

ON USING A FANCY BUTTER MOLD

If you happen to come across a pretty wooden butter mold, by all means, use it to display your butter to best advantage. A few hours before you make butter, submerge the butter mold in a pan of cold water. Water repels fat, so it's what you have to use to "grease" a container that's going to hold fat.

As soon as you finish washing your butter, shake the excess water off the butter mold and pack it full of soft butter, being careful to push the butter into any fancy carvings and all the corners. Scrape the excess butter off the top and chill the entire mold. When the butter is completely hard, turn the mold upside down on a plate and tap it a few times. The butter should release cleanly and slide right out.

it in your hands and knead it under running water, either in a bowl or your sink if it's clean enough, or on an angled board. There are trapped pockets of buttermilk in the butter, and if you don't work them all out, the buttermilk will sour unpleasantly and the butter will not keep well.

Doesn't it feel absolutely delightful to squeeze a couple of pounds of butter in your hands, instead of rationing out little bits from a foil-wrapped pat? When all the buttermilk is washed out, let the butter dry a bit, wrap it tightly in parchment, and refrigerate it. It's delicious right away, but if you let it age for a week or two in the refrigerator, it will only get better.

—R

Crème Fraîche

Exceedingly simple to make, crème fraîche is much more versatile than sweet cream. Not only can you whip it and serve it with desserts, but it has less of a tendency to curdle during cooking, and lends a delicate, sweet tang to everything you put it in. It also keeps better than sweet cream.

Take a jar, put in a quart of good, fresh (not ultra-pasteurized cream), and add a dollop of yogurt or buttermilk. Stir it well and leave it in a warm spot for a day or two (perhaps longer in winter) just until it thickens, at which point it's ready for cooking (or eating with a spoon!). Store in the refrigerator, where it will keep for a couple of weeks.

Ghee

Ghee is definitely divine—so pure, so deep, so nourishing, so versatile. I spread it on toast, serve it with roasted sweet potatoes, and put cartloads in my *dal*. I use it for deep-frying when making doughnuts for vegetarians, and give it away in little jars as presents. Unlike butter, it doesn't go rancid quickly, doesn't burn at high temperatures, and contains no lactose. Even in tiny quantities, it imparts an amazing depth of nutty caramel flavor to stews and baked goods. It's one of those "secret" old-fashioned ingredients that no shortcuts can imitate. Don't mistake it for clarified butter, either. Ghee cooks much longer than clarified butter, which is how it develops its nuttiness—the milk sugars slowly caramelize and infuse the ghee with their flavor before they're strained out.

Put a pound of butter over low heat in a heavy-bottomed wide pot. Monitor the heat closely to prevent even a hint of scorching, and let the butter slowly melt and sputter. Butter contains a lot of water and milk solids—it's far from being pure fat—and it takes a while for all that non-fat stuff to evaporate and separate. The milk solids start by forming a scum on the surface of the ghee and collecting on the bottom. As it caramelizes, the surface scum will be less foamy and more clumpy, and may settle to the bottom. Somewhere between 30 minutes and an hour (or even longer), the ghee will be completely separated and the scum will caramelize to a golden color. Under the scum, the liquid fat will appear completely clear. It's done.

When warm, ghee is a clear, golden oil.

Turn off the heat. Skim the scum from the surface. (Taste the scum—it will be delicious!)

Place a colander over a bowl and line it with several layers of cheesecloth. Pour the ghee through carefully. While it's still warm, ladle it into jars and refrigerate. It keeps well even at room temperature. Or pour it in a crock, cover it securely, dig a hole, and bury it underground to age for up to a hundred years. The flavor becomes more bitter as it ages, but its medicinal properties become more concentrated, according to traditional Ayurvedic teaching.

—*R*

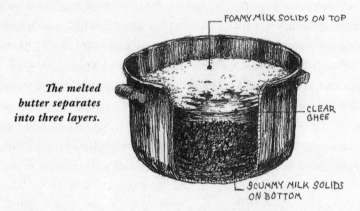

The melted butter separates into three layers.

FOAMY MILK SOLIDS ON TOP

CLEAR GHEE

SCUMMY MILK SOLIDS ON BOTTOM

Yogurt

This is it: Mama's simple, easy recipe for thick, custardy yogurt—no powdered-milk cheating, no fussy equipment. You can use a candy thermometer, or you can estimate the temperatures if you're good at recognizing a "hearty scald" and "yeast-water lukewarm." If lactose is problematic for you, you can dispel much of it if you culture the yogurt for 18 to 24 hours.

To start making yogurt, you'll need a little bit of starter yogurt for the live culture it contains. Look for plain, fresh live-culture yogurt with no additives—stabilizers and preservatives will hinder the bacterial culture and produce unpredictable results. I have gotten the best results with national brands like Nancy's. Some of the smaller artisan yogurt makers must have some very special, very needy cultures, because I can't get them to propagate consistently in my own yogurt.

You'll also need a gallon of good milk—and please do make sure it's good milk. Consider how much four quarts of yogurt would cost you in the grocery store. Spend that much on the milk for your yogurt, and you'll be five steps ahead. In my book, good milk is milk that's not homogenized, not skimmed, very fresh, and from cows that actually eat cow food: grass. But take care. While unhomogenized milk certainly makes a superior product—custardy, as opposed to gummy—it can also start turning into butter when vigorously shaken. I find that by the time I bike home with my milk, it has formed delicate yellow butter discs on top. I put these on my toast—unlike the cream, which can be stirred back into the milk, they will just melt when heated and form odd granules as they resolidify in the cooled yogurt. The cream, which rises to the top of full-fat non-homogenized milk, is essential to good yogurt and good health and must not be discarded.

Over a low flame, slowly heat the gallon of milk in a nonre-active pot to 180 degrees (a "hearty scald"—nice and foamy, like a heady beer, but no real simmering). Stir it occasionally as it heats, remembering that the faster you heat the milk, the more grainy bits of overheated congealed protein you'll find in your yogurt. When it's done, either just leave it in the pot and set outside to cool, with the lid off, or pour it into four quart jars. In any case, let it sit until cooled to 110 degrees ("yeast-water lukewarm"), at which point, take a spoonful of milk from each jar or pot, mix it with a spoonful of live-culture yogurt, and stir it back in. A tiny amount of yogurt can culture a large amount of milk. It just matters that it's well distributed in the milk. Lid the jars and place them in a lunch cooler as close together as possible. Fill two other jars with hot water and put them next to the yogurt. Pack towels around them, cover them up snug, and leave them for 24 hours.

You can also improvise with, say, a lightbulb in your oven. You can get a little lightbulb holder that plugs directly into an outlet and an extension cord for a few dollars at the hardware store. Depending on the insulation in your oven, you may need a higher or lower wattage. I go for 100 watts, which keeps my oven at a perfect 107 degrees. Don't ever, ever turn on the oven with an electric cord inside it! I recommend putting hyperbolic warning notes all over the oven.

You can also build a solar yogurt box with an old window— basically, an insulated wooden box with a glass lid. Put it in the sun and you'll be surprised how quickly it will warm up. It can easily get too warm, in fact—keep checking on it to keep the temperature regulated.

Don't disturb the yogurt while it's culturing. Refrain from jiggling the pot to see how thick it is. Let it take its good old time, too—24 hours. Refrigerate it when it's set. Always save a little yogurt for the next batch, provided you make it reasonably often—it starts to lose its culturing power after a week or so.

RAW MILK YOGURT

Raw milk yogurt has a delicate, complex, floral flavor, and the smoothest of custardy textures.

Slowly and gently heat the milk to 110 degrees, and no more. You won't even need a thermometer: just heat it till it feels a little warm when you put your finger in it. Add a little starter culture and proceed as with regular yogurt.

STRAINED (GREEK-STYLE) YOGURT

I resisted strained yogurt at first because it seemed so lavish and wasteful. You only end up with half the yogurt you start with—the rest drains out as whey. But it turns out that my boyfriend is addicted to whey as a light, refreshing beverage (he never has an appetite for breakfast if he doesn't have whey first thing), and substituting whey for water improves all baked goods, soups, and sauces. Straining yogurt isn't wasteful—it's efficient, dividing yogurt into its most versatile parts.

Make yogurt in a large pot, as suggested above. Place a colander over a large bowl, and line the colander with a couple of layers of fine cheesecloth. Ladle or pour in the yogurt, and let it drain for several hours, until the yogurt is half its former volume. You'll notice that the yogurt thickens and dries much more along the edges, where it can drain better, and you may be tempted to stir it all to even it out. There's no real problem in doing so, but if you leave it undisturbed, that dryer layer will peel away cleanly from the cheesecloth and you'll have less scraping work to do. Put the drained yogurt in a large bowl and beat it vigorously until smooth. Scoop it into a large jar and refrigerate.

Pour the whey into a glass jar, cover, and refrigerate. If well strained (quite free of cream or milk particles), it will keep for a good long time—several months or more.

Again, if you're going to use the yogurt to make another batch, do so within a week. You can also make yogurt with whey, but I haven't had to do that very often. Whey-cultured yogurt is slightly more tart and thin, but that won't much affect the new yogurt if you strain it, too.

If you decide to strain raw milk yogurt, you may find that the cream drains out with the whey. This is unacceptable for two reasons: first, the finished yogurt needs *all* its cream for deliciousness; and second, the cream makes the whey go bad more quickly than usual. If you find this happening, simply let the whey stand at room temperature in a wide bowl long enough for the cream to rise to the top—an hour or so. Skim it off with a ladle and stir it back into the strained yogurt.

—R

Cheese

Cheese-making is simple, and cottage cheese can be made by just adding something sour like lemon juice to milk, letting it curdle and pouring off the liquid whey or straining it through a wicker basket. In fact, the word *formaggio* in Italian comes from the simple draining basket. This is probably what the first Neolithic cheeses were like, so the story goes, curdled in a stomach bag container as an intrepid horseman trotted home from the field. Simple and fresh. But we are not after simple. We want the real thing: complex, tangy, herbaceous, aged, and ideally a little stinky. And for that you need rennet. Good milk helps too, preferably raw. People have been eating raw milk cheeses for ages and still do in Europe. In the United States, such cheeses can only be sold after aging, by which time any pathogens will be gone, so to play it safe, an aged cheese is a better option than simple and fresh. Here is a recipe to jump right into full-blown artisanal cheese-making, with practically no special equipment. Modern cheese-making supplies are not difficult to find online, and unless you buy a press, are relatively inexpensive. But cheese can really be made with nothing more than cheesecloth and a strainer.

A well-aged Cheddar cut in half.

CRACKING GOOD CHEESE

I call this cheese Stinkin' Lincoln. He was only named that because he was born on Lincoln's 200th birthday. Technically he is a kind of Cheddar. He is not difficult to make, but requires careful timing and about four or five hours of concentration. As Josiah Twamley, 18th-century English cheese expert and aficionado, wrote in his 1784 dissertation, *Dairying Exemplified*, "Cheese in general was made too much in a hurry." I have seasoned my own directions here with some of Twamley's astute observations.

First you will need just a few items of equipment. A thermometer is essential, as are cheesecloth and a big, fine-meshed colander. Expensive molds and a press can be bought for a lot of money, or you can devise a makeshift mold from what you have on hand. I used an inexpensive pasta pot with strainer insert. You can also use a plastic gallon-size milk jug. Cut off the top and poke holes in the bottom. I offer you a recipe that uses two gallons of milk, which is about right to get started. Smaller cheeses of this type dry out too quickly. If you have a really huge 20-quart stockpot, feel free to use three or four gallons—but that's about the upper limit that anyone can handle at home.

The only thing not easily obtained is rennet. You should buy this online from a cheese-making supply shop; it will arrive in a tiny bottle, packed and kept cold. I recommend real liquid rennet taken from the lining of a calf's stomach as traditional, but there does exist vegetable rennet, which Twamley points out was used in the 18th century by Jews who couldn't, because of their dietary laws, mix milk and meat. Animal rennet is more typical though, and I'm not sure one would get the same results using a vegetable version. In the past, people also used fig-tree sap for this purpose.

Most important, start with raw organic milk. I understand this is not always easy to obtain. Here in California and in many other states, it is perfectly legal. It is well worth hunting down online or via the Weston A. Price Foundation, which lists raw milk sources state by state on their website, westinaprice.org. In some states, you can buy a partial share in a cow, and thus as an "owner" can obtain raw milk from her legally. I won't ask how you find it, but I figure if you're going to the effort of making your own cheese, you don't want something that tastes like what you buy in the supermarket. If you absolutely cannot find raw milk, at least use organic milk, as it is likely to have some flavor.

Start by warming two gallons of milk to 90 degrees. Do this by putting the milk in your stockpot, covering it, and setting it in a sink filled with warm water. If the water's a little hotter than 90 degrees, it will warm up quicker; at 90 degrees it will take quite a while. Just don't overheat it or you'll damage or kill all the good bacteria you want alive. Most of the trick of this whole process is adding hot water gradually, letting some water drain out, over and over, to maintain a constant 90 degrees. You must maintain constant temperature carefully for the whole process. It's not difficult, just time-consuming. Remember, you are taking the temperature of the milk, not the water—which will cool over time, or warm up when you add hotter water. Be sure the milk is not too hot or, as Twamley says, you will have "Sweet, or Funkey Cheese."

When the milk is 90 degrees, add half a cup of live cultured buttermilk, which you can buy anywhere. Let it sit for an hour at 90 degrees.

Mix 20 drops of liquid rennet into 20 times the amount of cool water. About a cup is fine. Then pour into the milk and stir. Let this sit for about 45 minutes. Be sure not to disturb this in any way, or you may prevent coagulation. After 45 minutes, something magical happens: You will see that the curds have set, and it looks solid and perfectly coagulated. Not curdled—as you would see in milk gone bad, but a single jiggly mass.

With a long serrated bread knife, very gently cut the curds, still in the pot, into long thin slices, and then cut again across.

A pot containing cut curds floating in whey.

Don't break up the curds too much. Essentially what you have now are long vertical sticks. Let them sit for 20 minutes.

Add hotter water to the sink, until the temperature of the curds reaches 98 degrees. Hold it at this temperature for about half an hour. You will see the curds gradually sink to the bottom and stick together a bit. It will be ready when the whey is no longer white, but "you will always find the whey quite green," says Twamley. In fall, the whey may take on a bluish hue because the cows are no longer eating green grass.

Gently pour the mixture into a fine-meshed colander—a "China hat" shape works nicely. Try not to break up the curds violently or you will cause the fat to drain away; all you want is the greenish, watery whey to drip out. Let drain about 15 minutes or until the whey stops dripping. By the Way, keep the Whey!

Return the curds, which will now look like cottage cheese, back into your pot. Add two tablespoons of salt and stir to evenly distribute. Leave to rest for an hour. You'll see more whey exude.

Pour the curds into a cheesecloth-lined mold, and wrap them up like a little wheel or cylinder shape, depending on your mold. Use either a strainer basket, the perforated milk jug, or some other contraption here. Let the remaining whey drip down into the pot. Put a top on the cheese—I cut a circle of rigid plastic, but a small plate will work, too—and weigh it down. Start with a little weight on top and gradually increase until there's a lot of weight pressing down on the cheese. I did this by putting a water-filled glass jar on the plastic disk, and then a few hours later covered it with my granite mortar, which weighs about 40 pounds, upside down on top. Leave this to drain overnight.

Take the cheese out of the press and unwrap. It is born. Put it on a reed or bamboo mat—anything that allows the air to circulate underneath—in your cellar or cool storage area (I use the wine fridge) at about 50 to 55 degrees and turn a few times a day for two days.

Wrap the now firm and dry cheese in several layers of clean cheesecloth or thin muslin. Melt about a cup of lard and brush it all around the cheese, saturating the cloth. You can also brush the cheese with melted paraffin wax if you prefer.

Put it back in your cellar, wait 12 months. Then eat. You can actually eat it anytime after two or three months; the longer it sits, the sharper it will be. And remember, as long as you are doing this, feel free to double the recipe if you have vessels large enough.

—K

QUICK CHEESE

For those with little patience or who are unwilling to follow detailed recipes, a quick cheese can be made with less time and attention. In essence, you can "wing it" without a thermometer, timer, or anything. The result should be a perfectly delicious homemade cheese in just two weeks.

First, get a regular gallon of regular pasteurized whole milk and warm it right on the stove to nice baby bathwater temperature—you are going for 90 degrees. Add in about a quarter cup of yogurt with live active cultures, and let it sit for about an hour with the heat off. Add in about eight drops of rennet diluted in half a cup of cool water. Stir and let sit in the pot in a warm sink full of water. This takes about an hour, and the curds will be noticeably softer than the Cheddar recipe above. Cut the curds as instructed earlier, and add hot water to the sink, while letting the cooler water drain, until it is hot but not scalding. Let this sit for half an hour or more until you see whey separate from the curd. Salt, stir, and let sit again until the curds are completely separate and firm enough to pick up with your fingers. Then pour the curds into a fine-meshed strainer lined with cheesecloth. Let drain until fairly solidified, and weigh down right in the strainer over the sink or a large pot, overnight. In the morning you will have a soft mass that looks like cottage cheese but is firmer and stuck together in the shape of the strainer. Break this into four pieces and mold with your hands into round balls and let them sit in your cave about two weeks—a cool, dark place will do—when they will get firmer and develop flavor, though you can eat them immediately, too.

I have winged it on this recipe on separate occasions, sometimes using low-fat milk, sometimes using buttermilk, once being completely impatient with timing, and had wildly different results. Feel free to play with the recipe. Just keep in mind that a small cheese will dry out quickly, so if you want to age it a few weeks, it is best waxed or tightly wrapped. You can try wrapping it in a grape, fig, or sycamore leaf.

—K

RICOTTA

The day you make cheese, you will have a nice bucket of whey. Feed it to the pigs from which you will make prosciutto, or better yet, make ricotta. Ricotta means recooked in Italian, which in this case is not exactly accurate, since you haven't cooked anything yet, only warmed it. All the same. Ricotta is *not* cottage cheese! It is made from whey not milk. This confusion is nothing new though. Platina, the first librarian of the Vatican Library and dabbler in food writing, offers a nice 15th-century definition of *recocta* in *De honesta voluptate*, but first he says it's made from whey, then he says it's milk. "When the cheese is taken from the bronze kettle, we heat the whey for some time on a slow fire until the fat which is the residue of the cheese rises to the top. Farmers call it ricotta because it is gathered from the milk in a second heating" (Milham tr. 160–61).

You get the idea. Bring the whey up to a boil then lower the heat to medium. Little secondary curds will come to the top; skim them off. That's the ricotta. You can drain the whole thing into a colander if you lose patience skimming. Salt them lightly. You'll get about a cup of ricotta from two gallons of whey. If you make a bigger cheese, you'll have enough for a lasagne. Lasagne with your own tomato sauce, fresh noodles, and freshly made ricotta from raw milk—how can you do anything but faint? Or put the ricotta on a slice of toast from your own sourdough bread and drizzle with homemade *sapa* (boiled-down grape must). Same fainting procedure herewith.

RICOTTA GNOCCHI

To use your fresh ricotta, try making light, fluffy gnocchi. Take your ricotta and mix by hand with flour and a pinch of salt until it forms a soft paste. Add an egg and mix well. Roll by hand into little balls, and if you like, roll them over the edge of a fork to make little indentations. Drop these into boiling whey or water. When they float to the top, remove with a skimmer and set in a pan with gently bubbling butter (if you can get it from the same dairy source, all the better) and let them brown gently. Eat with just a few drops of lemon juice.

And now you're wondering: Is there something to do with the whey after this. *Yes!* Add it to the sourdough bread recipes instead of water. It gives it a beautiful tang and marvelous lift.

—K

10
Fermented Beverages

Like vegetables, fruits and cereals also ferment all on their own. In this case, sugars are converted to alcohol, and while practically any fruit can be fermented, it is the fruit of the vine that is accorded a special status in Western civilization. In the biblical version of the story, it is Noah who first plants grapes, makes wine, and proceeds to get drunk and naked. The Dionysian cults of ancient Greece were even more raucous.

Where grapes will not grow, people ferment cereal into beer—using barley, wheat, rice, and corn (though we refer to the latter two as rice wine in Asia and *pulque* in Mexico). Regardless of the origin, beer and wine have always been an integral part of civilized life.

The lovely thing about alcohol is that, just as our ancestors did, you can make your own without special equipment or hard-to-find ingredients. And even if you aren't patient enough for that, you can always use store-bought beer and wine for cooking up all sorts of traditional potions, sauces, and suppers.

Wine

Every year I make two or three bottles of wine. Here's why: The house I own was built in the 1920s by a Basque family that ran a restaurant in town. It has great cooking vibes and a monstrous old grape vine that stretches up over a trellis covering the entire patio. It is in fact why I bought the house. They are, alas, Concord grapes, which is fine if you like the flavor of Manischewitz. They do make a very nice verjuice—a medieval condiment made simply by squeezing unripe grapes, used much like lemon juice today. The ripe juice (called must) can also be boiled down for several hours to make *sapa*, a thick syrup used by the ancient Romans as a sweetener. It's also the base for balsamic vinegar. But wine is what I was after. So I decided to plant some vinifera grapes. At first I did everything by the book, using equipment, purchased yeast, and so forth. When all was done, I had something almost as good as what one can buy in a jug: drinkable, but only barely so. What's the point? What I really want is something unique, speaking directly of the soil, without modern equipment, without modern techniques, without even commercial yeast. Wine made as an ancient Greek might have done it. This is not something you can buy.

Here is how to do it: Crush your grapes either by hand or, if you are adventuresome, with your feet, and leave to ferment about two weeks covered loosely with a cloth. The natural wild yeast already on the grapes does all the work. The muck on top has to be pushed under a few times a day. Then the whole thing is strained through a cheesecloth-lined sieve, squeezed hard to remove as much liquid as possible, and bottled. An ancient Greek amphora is ideal. A month to age and you may have a bouquet redolent of newspaper and gym socks, but it will be yours. I've done it every year, about a jugful or two, and either I'm getting a little better at doing this or my taste buds are deteriorating. The bottle I opened last year at a party was drunk happily. It has to be decanted, and strained at the end like port, because there is a crust.

WINE IN RECIPES

If you are not interested or able to make your own wine, there are many interesting things that one can do with store-bought wine. We tend to think that if you do anything to wine it is adulteration. In the past, people had no such concerns. They added water to wine, which often improves it, and regularly added spices and herbs. Maywine, flavored with woodruff, is one example, from Germany, sometimes still found for sale. Drinks like vermouth are the only remaining members of a once huge tribe of medicinal fortified wines. There is no reason not to try to make these at home.

I offer one recipe for the modern devotee, another very ancient indeed. The historic versions are usually called *hipocras*, with vague allusion to the father of medicine, Hippocrates. Here it is called *Conditum paradoxum*, taken from the cookbook attributed to the ancient Roman Apicius. I have reduced all the quantities by one-fifth, since the original makes buckets upon buckets. Mastic is a tree resin from the Greek Isle of Chios and can be bought in a Greek grocery. It is the familiar flavor of retsina; long ago, the flavor would come from the pitch lining the amphorae of wine.

CONDITUM PARADOXUM FROM APICIUS

Take 3 pounds of honey [three jars] and put it in a bronze vessel with eight ounces of wine [a big glassful], and cook the honey and wine together, heated on a small fire of dry wood, stirring with a stick while it cooks. If it boils, pour in some wine to settle it, or just move from the fire. When it's cooled, put it back again. Do this a second then third time, and then remove from the fireplace and after a day skim it, then add ¾ ounce of pepper already ground [4½ teaspoons], about half an ounce of mastic, a bay leaf and a pinch of saffron, 1 toasted date pit and the date itself softened in wine,* the same kind as before and the same amount, and pounded to smooth paste. When all of this is done, add in 72 ounces of dry wine [about three bottles].

*Pound the date and its pit in a cup of wine taken from the three bottles, and the proportions will be perfect.

Psychic Love Wine

This is a similar spiced wine redolent of the Middle Ages. Take a one-and-a-half-liter bottle of dry white wine, nothing expensive of course. Sauvignon blanc or cheap pinot grigio is fine. Heat the wine gently in a pot and add to it an array of spices, including pepper, cinnamon, ginger, nutmeg, mace, aniseed, coriander, lemon peel—anything you like. Just try to avoid the pumpkin-spice combo of cloves, nutmeg, and cinnamon, which is too sweet and cloying on its own. You really want this to be spicy with ginger hot in the mouth. If you can find long pepper, cubeb, grains of paradise, cassia buds, spikenard, or other medieval spicery, go ahead. Most can be found online. They are amazing. A drop of rosewater is nice, too.

Add a dash of honey to temper its heat and cook gently without letting it boil, for about half an hour. Let cool and add one or two cups of brandy to the mixture. You need to do this, since some alcohol will have burned off. Feel free to add more if you like. Keep this in a vessel undisturbed for at least a week, spices and all. You can pour it back into the original wine bottle, though you'll have a little extra. When it tastes rounded and mellow, decant into another bottle, straining out the spices. Chill in the fridge or serve at room temperature. This will completely shatter everyone's conception of Christmasy mulled wine. This is, incidentally, an aphrodisiac.

—K

Beer

If you would like to become a crafter of beer, there are many resources available to you, from books to the Internet. You will make many friends—including me—and shouldn't be afraid to enlist our aid when it's time to scrub your brewing equipment down.

But the modern approach to beer-making can be a little unsatisfying. Most home-brewers start out with malt extract. They boil it, add hops, put in the right yeasts, and let it ferment. Purists use real malt, which they buy from a brewing supply store. This adds a couple of steps to the process, giving the purists cleaner, deeper flavors, and more satisfaction when they tap the keg. But when I asked if any had ever made their

There's an old English folk song that tells the tale of ale-making from the perspective of the much-abused barley grain (known as a "corn" before *corn* came to specify maize).

It paints a vivid picture of the traditional harvesting and brewing process.

John Barleycorn

There were three men come from the West
Their fortunes for to try,
And these three made a solemn vow:
"John Barleycorn must die."

They plowed, they sowed, they harrowed him in,
Threw clods upon his head,
Till these three men were satisfied
John Barleycorn was dead.

They let him lie for a very long time,
Till the rains from heaven did fall,
When little Sir John raised up his head
And so amazed them all.

They let him stand till Mid-Summer's Day
When he looked both pale and wan;
Then little Sir John grew a long, long beard
And so became a man.

They hired men with their scythes so sharp
To cut him off at the knee;
They rolled him and tied him around the waist,
And served him barbarously.

They hired men with their sharp pitchforks
To pierce him to the heart,
But the loader did serve him worse than that,
For he bound him to the cart.

They wheeled him round and around the field
Till they came unto a barn,
And there they took a solemn oath
On poor John Barleycorn.

They hired men with their crab-tree sticks
To split him skin from bone,
But the miller did serve him worse than that,
For he ground him between two stones.

There's little Sir John in the nut-brown bowl,
And there's brandy in the glass,
And little Sir John in the nut-brown bowl
Proved the strongest man at last.

The huntsman cannot hunt the fox
Nor loudly blow his horn
And the tinker cannot mend his pots
Without John Barleycorn.

— *Traditional*

own malt, I was scoffed off the scene. I didn't understand why—malt is simply grain, usually barley, sprouted to just the right point before it's carefully dried at low temperatures and ground. I went to work.

This is a recipe for cottage beer, the sort of beer you can brew entirely from scratch without fancy equipment of any sort, but can vary to your endless amusement. You can brew it strong and drink it at night, or brew it weak and quaff it for breakfast. You can make it hoppy or not, you can toast some of the grains, you can throw in a bit of ginger or raisins—however you like. There may be some batches you'd rather cook with than drink, and some you'd rather drink alone than share with guests. But however it goes, it will be a fizzy, malty beverage.

Yeast turns sugar into alcohol and carbon dioxide. So the first step in any alcohol-making endeavor is preparing the sugar (in the case of beer, sugar comes from the malt). Unlike fruit, grain locks up its sugars in the form of starch for storage—the brewer has to coax the sugars out. First, you unlock starch-digesting enzymes by partially sprouting the grain (malting). Then you let those starch-digesting enzymes go to work on the starches (mashing). The sugars dissolve in the liquid (wort) when it's strained out of the grains, and boiling concentrates the sugars to a good potency. Hops go in during the boiling phase, too. After that, the liquid cools to a yeast-friendly temperature, the yeast goes in, and the fermentation starts. Once the yeast eats most of the sugar, the brew is bottled or kegged. A little extra sugar in the bottle gives the yeast something to chew on in the dark, and makes the brew fizzy when you open it.

These directions are for a very small batch of beer—one gallon. The large scale of most brewing is what makes it difficult. I recommend making a small batch before scaling up. And after making a batch or two, you'll know what to expect and you'll know what pieces of equipment to look for. You could purchase real airlocks, large glass carboys, or a grain mill. Grinding grain with a mortar and pestle is a pain.

MALTING

Barley makes a very nice beer, of course, but a little wheat in the mix will give it a good, foamy head. Don't, however, attempt to sprout barley and wheat at the same time: barley is much larger and requires more time to both sprout and dry. Look for unhulled barley—pearled barley has been subjected to too much abuse for it to sprout anymore. Dried, whole malt keeps well, so go ahead and make as large a batch as you can conveniently dry in one go.

Soak a pound of grain overnight in a half-gallon jar full of water. In the morning, drain and rinse it and tie cheesecloth

All of these barley grains are ready to dry. Note that the tiny sprout is hidden beneath the husk on some of these grains. Peel the husk away to see the sprout growing down the side of the grain—unlike the rootlets, which grow away from the grain.

over the mouth of the jar. Let the jar rest, propped at an angle in a bowl so extra moisture can run out the mouth of the jar. Rinse it morning and evening for a few days, watching the grain closely. Thin rootlets will grow away from the grain, while a single sprout will grow down the side of the grain. It is the sprout you want to pay attention to—which will be tricky with barley, where the hull obstructs your view. When the sprouts are the length of the grain, no more and no less, dry them immediately. If the weather is warm, sprouts can quickly grow past the optimal sugar stage. Spread them out in a thin layer on a sheet tray and put them in the oven at no more than 150 degrees. Keep the oven door ajar for air circulation. I dry mine while making yogurt, so the temperature is only 110. You can also dry them outside on a hot day. Depending on the ambient humidity, they may take a day or two to dry.

When the grains are completely light and crunchy-dry, you may store them in a jar until you need them. If you'd like some darker flavors in your beer, toast a portion of the grain in a 350-degree oven after it dries, until golden-brown. But don't toast all of it, or you'll destroy the enzymes that unlock sugars for you.

GRINDING

You'll have to crack the malted grain to make beer. This is quite the chore without a grain grinder. Perhaps you can find somebody with a mill—a good brewing supply store, the hippie next door, or your grandma. A coffee mill might work, but don't make it run very long, or it will heat the grains too much. And don't grind the grain too fine. It should be just cracked, not powdery at all, or else the beer will be sludgy and cloudy.

If it comes down to it, just get to work in a large mortar and pestle. A heavy rolling pin on a tabletop also works. Don't try to crack more than a sprinkling of grains at a time, allow yourself an hour or two, and put on some music. You only need to crack the grain coarsely, and the hulls will more or less stay in one piece.

MASHING

The enzymes that transform starch into sugar work best between 140 and 160 degrees. You'll want to hold the malt in a soupy bath at that temperature for an hour. If you don't have a thermometer, I find that water at 140 degrees is hot enough that I can put my finger in it for only a few seconds, but not so hot that it hurts to touch it right away. For a pound of barley malt and four ounces of wheat malt, use half a gallon of water. Keep it warm in a turned-off oven or just bundle it in towels. Ladle the mash into a cheesecloth-lined strainer over a large bowl and let it drain slowly into a large pot. Leave the grains where they are in the colander over the large pot. Heat another half gallon of water to 150 degrees, and slowly pour that through the grains (this is called sparging, and rinses out extra sugars). You should now have about three-quarters of a gallon of liquid in the large pot.

BOILING

You will probably have less than a gallon of wort (malt-sugary liquid) now. That's fine. Bring it to a boil and add a scattering of dried hops. You can find dried hops in the herb section of a well-stocked grocery store, in a brewing supply store, or online (see Resources). In total, you'll need about a quarter of an ounce of hops, which you add in two or three stages during an hour of boiling. Hops added at the beginning of boiling will add bitterness to the beer, while hops added toward the end give it good aromas. The last of the hops should go in when you turn off the heat. Simply let them steep for five minutes. If you don't have hops, you can use a cleaned dandelion plant—roots, leaves, flowers, and all. The boiling not only serves the purposes of hops, but also concentrates and gently caramelizes the malt sugars.

Pour the wort through a cheesecloth-lined colander to strain out the hops, and then funnel it into a narrow-necked gallon jug, which is to be your fermentation vessel. If your fermentation vessel is glass, take some care, as glass will crack when put in contact with hot liquid. Since you probably boiled off a good quantity of liquid, just pour some cool water in the bottom of the jug, and slowly pour the warm wort into the water, without touching the glass walls of the jug. When you've put in all the wort, add water to fill the jug nearly up to the neck. Touch the side of the jug. When it feels barely warm to the touch, you're ready to ferment.

FERMENTING

There are many kinds of yeast, some of which work better than others. I do not recommend commercial baker's yeast. I often use sourdough starter, which I prime for several days beforehand by feeding it twice a day on white flour. Since I made my starter in San Francisco, there's probably a little *Lactobacil-*

lus sanfranciscensis in my culture, which gives the beer a sour zing. Thankfully, my boyfriend has a penchant for sour beer. The thing to remember, if contamination is your pet fear, is that the sugary wort you have prepared is yeast food. Mold does not get along well with the alcohol yeast quickly produces. (For that matter, the lactobacilli in sourdough culture produce an antibiotic that kills non-yeast organisms.)

Brewing supply stores, on land and on the Internet, have a vast selection of yeasts, which will each impart special characteristics to your brew. The most notable differences are between top-fermenting and bottom-fermenting yeasts. The former, which bubble and froth at the top of the ferment, give birth to sweeter ales, while the latter produce lagers. Of course, the only way those yeasts came to be so specialized was from folks who just went to work with the yeasts they had at hand and saved the strains. Apart from bacterial colonization (which is a serious problem), contamination is really just a matter of not getting exactly what you aimed at. For instance, *Brettanomyces*, a yeast that is considered a contaminant in English ales, is celebrated in certain Belgian brews.

You, too, can save and reuse your yeast. As it reproduces rapidly during fermentation, a yeast slurry forms on the bottom of the jug (the lees). Refrigerate it as soon as primary fermentation is complete, as it will quickly start to cannibalize itself, producing a nutrient-rich medium for bacterial growth. If you don't want to use it for brewing again, dry it and sprinkle it on your popcorn for some B-vitamin goodness.

To pitch the yeast, I simply let a quarter cup or so dribble through the funnel. Remove the funnel, cap the jug tightly, and give it a good vigorous shake, which both distributes the yeast and aerates the wort. Check to see how full your fermenting vessel is. It should have a couple of inches of head room. Add water if you need to. Cap the jug with an airlock, or just a balloon. Both airlocks and balloons allow carbon dioxide to bubble out but don't let contaminants in. If you use a balloon, be sure to unseal it every so often when it starts to inflate, or it will fly away on its own power (yes, some contaminants could sneak in while you unseal it, but it's better than nothing). If you try to seal the jug at this stage, you will get explosions. Very messy.

Soon, foam and bubbles will appear. As the days go by, the beer will form a thick froth, and you'll be able to watch all the bubbles floating toward the surface. Let it foam and bubble until it's all bubbled out—this may, depending on the temperature and sugar content, take several days to more than a week. The beer is done with its primary fermentation when the yeast has consumed all the sugar, and you see no more bubbles rising to the surface.

BOTTLING

The idea is to transfer the liquid in your fermentation vessel to a bowl, add sugar, and then transfer that to your bottles, all the while disturbing the liquid as little as possible. You also want to leave behind the yeasty sludge on the bottom of the fermentation vessel. Any oxygen introduced at this stage will cause oxidation and off-flavors. The easiest method is to make a siphon. A siphon is nothing more than a two-foot piece of food-grade flexible tubing about a centimeter thick. Place your fermentation vessel on top of a table, and put your bowl on the seat of a chair. Stick one end of the tubing into the brew and suck on the other end like it's a straw, just until you taste the

SLUDGE

Hold your thumb over the free end of the hose, taking care to keep its other end above the level of the sludge in the fermenting vessel.

brew. Quickly slip your thumb over the end of the tube to hold the seal, and put the end of the tube in the bowl. Slide your thumb off, still holding the tube, and let the liquid drain into the bowl. Make sure the end of the tube in the fermentation jug stays under the level of the liquid, but above the level of the yeast-sludge (the lees).

Add about a tablespoon of sugar per quart of liquid (you should have a gallon—four quarts), depending on how much carbonation you want. The yeast will consume this sugar inside the sealed bottles—just as they did in the open carbonation vessel. This time, the carbon dioxide they produce will be trapped inside the liquid, giving it fizz. Stir the sugar in gently. As with all stages of the brewing process, be clean, but by now there should be enough alcohol in your brew to mitigate the impact of any contaminants.

Repeat the siphoning process, this time from the bowl to your bottles or keg. I prefer using swing-top bottles, such as what Grolsch comes in, as then I don't have to worry about getting a bottle capper.

Let the beer age in a dark place for at least two weeks and ideally a month before sampling it. It will taste much better—mellower and richer. Save the lees for yeasting your next batch of beer!

It really helps to keep records of each batch you make. Write down the quantities you used, your methods, temperatures, and timings. Unless you never want to make the same brew twice.

—R

Cooking with Beer

Beer also makes an excellent cooking ingredient, lending its malty hoppiness to other dishes—that is if you can tolerate the idea of not drinking it. Be sure to accompany these dishes with the same beer that went into the food.

SWAZI SAUCE

I have long ago left behind my bold beer-swilling youth. But in college, I did my duty, even collecting labels from a marvelous pub in DC, the Brickskeller, which boasted beers from around the world. I was determined to try them all. It was then, too, that I learned to cook with beer, taking my cue initially from my roommate, who relished Cap'n Crunch doused in a cold brewsky for breakfast. But the first proper beer recipe I learned came from a friend of ours from Swaziland, who insisted that

KETCHUP

Slowly simmer a pot of roughly cut tomatoes, skin, seeds, and all, until they break down. Pass them through a food mill into another pot, add a cup of vinegar, a cup of sugar, a little ground clove, salt, and grated onion. All this is to taste. Add herbs, too, if you like, but the effect should not be tomato sauce–like, so go light on the oregano and basil. Cook this down on the lowest possible heat as long as you can until thick. It's ketchup!

this was the authentic barbecue sauce used there—where a barbecue is called a *braai*. Authentic or not, it is a template upon which dozens of superb sauces may be based.

First and most important, there must be beer, the good stuff. Back then my favorite was Old Peculier, but a decent pale ale works wonders. Then a glop of ketchup; a good dash of Tabasco; and a dribble of honey, lemon, and pepper. The proportions are utterly unimportant. Like you, I have serious doubts about its origins, but it is delicious. Feel free to mess with the contents. Since we are striving for antiquation, begin by making your own ketchup.

Proceed to make your barbecue sauce, substituting ingredients at whim. Use jam instead of honey—something like raspberry, or even maple syrup if you're doing pork. Cumin can substitute for pepper, a real chopped chili pepper, lime juice, maybe onion, and crushed garlic. Never garlic powder—fetid stuff. Otherwise, the contents really do not matter. The only indispensable ingredient is the beer.

What you do with Swazi Sauce does matter. Marinate chicken pieces in it, at least two hours before throwing on the grill. Cook the chicken on a very low flame, or the sugars in the sauce will burn. It also works splendidly with pork ribs, and even grilled vegetables. The only thing to keep in mind is to use very low heat, with the grill top off, and long, slow cooking. Baste with the marinade as you go, using it all up, but be sure not to use the sauce in which you marinated the meat as a dipping sauce. Make some fresh if you like to serve with sauce.

BEER BREAD

Beer also works very nicely in bread, which makes perfect sense, since it is essentially liquid bread. Use something extremely strong and hoppy, because you really do want the beer flavor to come through. Belgian Trappist Ale is excellent for beer bread. The only thing to keep in mind is that the alcohol content in the beer will slow down the yeast, so it may take a little longer to rise, but should not be a problem. Otherwise, use beer instead of water in the standard sourdough recipe. (See chapter five for bread recipes.) Instead of four or five hours to rise, leave it overnight for about eight hours and never punch it down. The resulting texture has large uneven holes, and a serious bitter hoppy bite that is a marvelous counterpoint to sweet butter. It also makes a great sandwich with corned beef or pastrami.

You can also make a delightful rye bread with beer. Simply mix equal parts dark rye flour and bread flour (two cups of each makes a nice-size bread), add proofed yeast, caraway seeds and enough beer to make a wet dough, and a bit of salt. Strangely, don't knead this; just let it rise on a baking sheet for about two hours or more. It will spread out a bit. Bake at 400 degrees until browned and sounds hollow when thumped, about 30 minutes.

—K

Beer Stews and Other Pleasant Diversions

Beer can be used in place of water or wine in a stew. Guinness and beef is classic. There's also the infamous "beer-can chicken"—the open can rammed into the bird from behind, set upright in the barbecue, and cooked, or rather gently steamed in the beer. I would like to suggest some unorthodox uses for beer in cookery, or at least some combinations that make gastronomic sense. The rule of thumb here is to match the cuisine with the country from which the beer originates. For example, Swazi Sauce (page 184), made with Foster's, would go very nicely with a slab of grilled barramundi. Or Sapporo in a tempura batter, using mushrooms, cauliflower, carrot, and so forth, and served with soy and wasabi.

Here is an idea for a simple braised stew with beer. It is sort of a Spanish *cocido*, and if you can find Spanish beer, by all means use it. We rarely think of Spain as a beer-drinking country, but envision the Visigothic kings who ruled after the fall of Rome and maybe it will make more sense. In any park in Madrid, you can find people sipping beer and munching on huge bowls of green olives, which is where this idea originated.

Start with lamb stew meat. Brown small pieces in olive oil and remove from the pan and set aside. Add to the pan a sliced onion and a sliced red pepper and cook until these are wilted. Put the lamb back in the pot and add in a handful of pitted green olives. Season with salt, pepper, tarragon, and some *Pimentón de la Vera* (smoked paprika). Add beer so ingredients are barely covered, lower heat, and simmer until lamb is tender, an hour or longer. Add more beer as necessary.

Another idea: Deep-fried beer-battered fish can be a lovely thing, but infinitely more interesting is fish gently poached in beer. I suggest something approximating a herring, or even a salmon filet, poached gently in a court bouillon of *weissbier*, which has a nice lemony yeasty aroma, with a sprig of dill, chopped carrot, and a little onion. After about five minutes, remove the fish, turn up the heat to reduce the beer stock by half, add a little butter, and drizzle over the fish to serve. If you like thick sauces, you can add a pinch of flour. Garnish with raspberries. Yes!

—*K*

11
Pies, Pastry, and Other Confections

The making of sweets ought to be a joyful and celebrative thing. In the days before rampant diabetes, metabolic syndrome, and cancer, sugar and refined flour were rare and expensive commodities. Less expensive were butter and eggs, particularly for rural cooks. And good fresh fruit was dirt cheap—it grew on trees. Nowadays, this hierarchy of expense has been turned almost completely upside-down, with mass-produced sugar and refined flours ranking among the cheapest edible substances on the planet. Sugar has found its way into everything, from fancy extruded breakfast cereals to tooth-aching "cocktails" and lattes, from high-tech sports drinks to ketchup. Our palates have become jaded—and we have gotten sick.

The saddest part is that most of this sugar-laden junk tastes like crap. It does. It's nothing but vacuous puffed nonsense, cheap chemical syrups, and stale gummy crumbs laced with preservatives.

I firmly believe that the only sweets worth eating are the ones made by a skilled and temperate baker—preferably you.

These sweets showcase the abundance of seasonal fruit or the bold flavors of unrefined sweeteners like maple syrup and molasses. They have plenty of good butter, eggs, and cream to satiate the appetite and add nutritional value, and they don't cater to jaded palates. Their textures are intriguing, delicate, flaky, and smooth; their subtlety can stop the most voracious pig in his tracks and force him to slowly savor the beauty of the baker's craft. No other sort of sweet is worth its sugar.

Pastry for Pies

Pastry-making is harder than it used to be. Old-fashioned cultured butter is somewhat acidic, which helps break down the gluten in flour and makes for more tender pastries. To compensate, this recipe uses whey for its liquid, as well as an egg for lightness. The butter gets broken in coarsely by hand, and the dough is folded in quarters to create many layers of butter. It's not difficult, and the results are magnificent.

This recipe makes four large, incredibly flaky crusts—enough for two double-crust pies, or four open-face pies, with some extra. You can easily freeze what you don't immediately need.

In a large bowl, whisk together five cups of flour and a tablespoon of fine sea salt. You can use pastry flour, all-purpose flour, or even bread flour if it's all that you've got.

In a small bowl, whisk together an egg and a quarter cup of whey. If you don't have whey on hand, use a tablespoon of apple cider vinegar and three tablespoons of ice water. Have an additional mug of ice water at the ready.

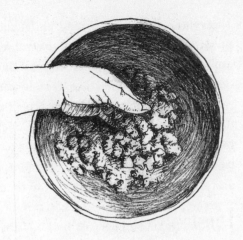

The largest butter chunks should be the size of marbles.

Using your fingers, briskly pinch a pound of cold butter (cultured, if you can) into the salted flour. The goal is to have a variety of butter chunks, ranging from little crumbles to marbles, all malleable but not warm. Merely slicing the butter will give you square chunks that won't properly flatten into a billion flaky layers when you go to roll out the dough. Every so often, plunk both hands in the flour and feel out the largest pieces. Quickly rub these between your fingers to make smear-crumbles. The whole process should take just a few minutes, and it's okay if you feel a little slatternly—soon everything will be in order. You're done when none of the butter chunks are much larger than marbles.

Drizzle the egg mixture into the flour, fluffing frequently with a fork, until mostly distributed. Continue drizzling with ice water and fluffing until most of the mixture is in lumps but a fair bit of it is still loose and crumbly. Divide the dough into quarters, pat each quarter into a crumbly ball, cover, and refrigerate for an hour or so.

Lightly flour your rolling surface and remove one dough-portion from the fridge. With the rolling pin, pat it down, packing it until it holds together, and roll the dough, from the center outward, into a 10-inch disc. Gently fold the dough in half, and then in half again. Re-flour your rolling surface, and roll the dough a second time into a large circle, checking frequently to be sure the dough isn't sticking. Fold the dough in half and transfer it into your pie dish. Unfold it, push it into the corners, and trim any excess hanging more than an inch over the edge. Use the trimmings to patch any thin or torn areas.

If making a single-crust pie, fold the overhanging rim to lie flush with the dish, press it together, and flute it. If making a double crust, just leave it as is. Cover the crust loosely and return to the refrigerator. Repeat with the remaining crusts. When rolling out the dough for a lattice top, you may find it simpler to fold the dough in thirds, like a letter, before rolling it the second time, since it doesn't need to be circular.

Pastry freezes well, so you can line a pie dish, wrap it up well, and stash it in the freezer for another day.

ATTACHING THE TOP CRUST

First, the bottom crust needs to hang over the edge of the pie pan by about three-quarters of an inch. After placing your filling inside the bottom crust, dab the overhanging rim of the bottom crust with water. Place the top crust over the filled pie and trim it to be half an inch smaller than the bottom crust all the way around. Fold the edge of the bottom crust back up over the rim of the top crust, pressing it firmly to seal. Flute the edge and bake right away (see page 194).

MAKING A LATTICE

Lay all the strips going in one direction before placing the first crosswise strip in the center. Weave it under every other strip.

You'll want to have all your dough strips ready *before* you fill the pie, so the bottom crust doesn't have time to get soggy. Using a pizza wheel or a sharp knife, cut the rolled-out dough for the top crust into strips about half an inch wide, or whatever you prefer. Fill the pie, and dab the overhanging rim of the bottom crust with water. Arrange all the vertical strips about half an inch apart across the pie.

Lay the first horizontal strip down the middle of the pie. Starting from the middle and working outward, lift every other vertical strip and place the horizontal strip under it. Put the second horizontal strip next to the first and again working from the center, run it under all the vertical strips you didn't go under last time. Continue to within half an

Continue placing crosswise strips, working out from the center and weaving each one before placing the next.

*Fold the overhanging rim
of the bottom crust over the
ends of the strips.*

*Flute the rim by pressing it
between your thumbs and
index fingers.*

inch of the edge of the pie. Trim the ends of the lattice strips to be about half an inch shorter than the bottom crust.

Fold the overhanging rim of the bottom crust up over the ends of the lattice. There may be thick spots where two lattice strips meet right at the edge of the pie. Trim them to even it out as best you can, and use the trimmings to fill in any thin spots where there are no lattice strips. Press the rim firmly and flute. Bake immediately.

—R

Pie Fillings

There's a lingering hint of ancient gnomish magic in the crafting of lidded hidden fastened things. That's why dumplings and pies and sushi and burritos and other rolled-away, tucked-in, balled-up edibles are so remarkably appealing. More often than not, the bulk of the labor is in the wrapping of our edible packages—the fillings are a simple chop–chop–sauté or a pare–core–toss. But after all, they are the point—and often as not, the meat—of the matter.

Here are some guidelines on the gems in the treasure chest, the pastry-cloaked mysteries of old.

FRUIT PIES

A fruit pie requires just sweetener (usually sugar) and thickener, tossed with the raw fruit. To know how much sweetener and thickener your fruit will need, taste it. How sweet or moist is it? Apples, for example, are quite dry, but range in sweetness from tart Granny Smith to sweet Golden Delicious. Choose firmer, drier varieties when baking. Sour cherries are juicy but not very sweet. Peaches are both juicy and so sweet they might want some lemon juice to perk them up. Berries, likewise, are sweet and juicy (with the exception of tart ground-cherries; wine berries and black raspberries; and dry, tart cranberries). Rhubarb is dry but extremely tart. Extremely tender, seedy fruits like raspberries are probably better on a fresh fruit tart, or added for accent to peaches.

Tart fruits will require about a cup of sugar per pie's worth of fruit, and moist fruits will take about four tablespoons cornstarch, tapioca, or flour to thicken. Sweet fruits like apples need only a few tablespoons of sugar, and dry fillings like rhubarb need just a tablespoon of thickener.

Many fruits come with their own set of traditional pairings. Apples take a teaspoon or more of cinnamon and a pinch of nutmeg. Stone fruits like peaches and cherries do very well with a drop of almond extract and a splash of brandy or bourbon. Try nutmeg and vanilla with blackberries, and ginger with peaches or rhubarb. Squeeze in a bit of lemon if your fruit isn't naturally tart, and don't forget to pinch in a bit of salt. Above all, the quality of your fruit is its greatest seasoning. Mealy, imported, out-of-season peaches will make a mealy, imported, out-of-season pie. Appearances, of course, matter much less—so make pie out of all the blemished produce you can find.

To prepare the fruit, wash it and remove any pits or cores. Peeling is optional—but do be sure to dice your fruit finely if you include the peels, so they're less obtrusive in the finished pie. Slice large fruit and pile it in your empty pie dish to estimate the amount you'll need, accounting for the fact that the fruit will shrink significantly in the oven. Dump it into a large bowl and add the appropriate amount of sweets, thickeners, and seasonings. Let it macerate while you roll out the top crust.

Dark- and bright-colored pies are beautiful under a lattice top (see Making a Lattice, page 193), but a simple top crust is lovely, too, and works especially well for drier fruits like apples (see Attaching the Top Crust, page 192). Don't try to make a fruit pie without any kind of top; it's liable to turn dry and leathery.

Fruit pies do well when baked in a hot oven to start. For the first 20 minutes or so, bake them around 450 degrees. Then reduce the oven temperature to prevent the crust from browning too much and continue baking at 350 until thick juices bubble in the middle—about an hour more, depending on the size of the pie.

SQUASH CUSTARD PIES

The most famous custard pie is pumpkin. Other winter squash pies (butternut, delicata, acorn, hubbard) are nearly indis-

TO WHIP CREAM

Immediately before serving, pour a cup of cold heavy whipping cream in a deep, medium-size bowl with a tablespoon of sugar or maple syrup and a long splash of vanilla. Whip with a whisk till it holds soft peaks. The cream will roughly double in volume, and is probably enough for eight servings of pie.

A whisk, by the way, is vastly preferable to an electric beater. First, the time saved by using electricity is insignificant, and completely negated by the time it takes to set up and clean up the beater. Second, a whisk is much less disruptive to after-dinner conversation. And finally, it's much harder to overwhip your cream with a whisk—hand-whipped cream is lighter and more delicate than electric cream.

tinguishable from pumpkin if you apply the same spicing formula. You can, in fact, use all sorts of mashed vegetables, provided they are the kind that get very tender when cooked. Sweet potatoes and parsnips are two sterling examples. Oddly, plain custard pie is less common these days, and I am content with that. Pastry and plain custard require very different baking methods, and I would rather have them separate.

Start with at least two pounds of your chosen vegetable. Wash them well. Pumpkins and squash need to be cut in half and deseeded, but potatoes and parsnips can be roasted whole. Roasting concentrates flavor and drives out moisture. You would much rather have the moisture in your custard come from something creamy, like milk, than watery vegetables, which encourage curdling. Place them in a greased baking dish with cut-side down, add a bit of water, and put them in a hot oven until velvety-tender. Add more water as needed, to keep the mixture from drying out.

Scoop the flesh out of its skin and let it cool. Measure what you need for your pie and freeze the rest. You may put the roast vegetable through your food mill, beat it with a rotary beater, or simply mash it with a potato masher or fork until it's reasonably smooth. No disasters will occur if it's lumpy. Freeze any puree that you don't need immediately; it keeps quite well.

To make the pie, line a nine-inch fairly deep pie plate with a single pastry shell. Put it somewhere cold while you make the custard. Preheat the oven to 400.

The basic ratio: two cups roasted, mashed vegetable; three-quarters cup good, rich milk; half a cup sour cream or crème fraîche; two eggs; two-thirds cup of sugar or other sweetener; a pinch of salt; and your spices.

Pumpkin pie spices (these apply to winter squash and sweet potato pies, too): one teaspoon ground cinnamon, three-quarters teaspoon ground ginger, half teaspoon grated nutmeg, quarter teaspoon ground cloves. At least half the sugar should be brown sugar. Or use half a cup of honey and one to two tablespoons of blackstrap molasses.

Parsnip pie spices: half a teaspoon ground cinnamon, quarter teaspoon ground nutmeg, and one-eighth teaspoon ground cloves. Use only maple syrup for the sweetener.

Beat the mixture vigorously and let it sit for a few minutes before you pour it in the pie shell. Bake at 400 for 15 minutes, then reduce the oven temperature to 325 and continue baking until the custard has risen around the edges but still jiggles a bit in the middle. The custard will continue to set after you remove it from the oven. Let it cool.

Serve with whipped cream. Store custard pies in the fridge.

PECAN PIE

You might consider pecan pie a custard pie because of its egg content. But without the milkiness, it has an entirely different effect on the tongue.

A decade ago, I had only to tromp down the steep, twisting cellar stairs and brush away the cobwebs to get a gallon or two of maple syrup from our vast stores. Papa had a thriving sugarbush (converted livestock trough) when we lived in West Virginia, producing some 30 gallons of maple syrup a year. We drenched our Sunday pancakes and flooded the yawning cavities of our Sunday waffles. We compared vintages and hues, and learned how to wash sticky crystals of maple out of my shepherdess-length hair. If you don't have maple syrup in such abundance, dates can help you stretch what you've got.

The night before you bake, soak a cup and a half of raw pecans in salted water to cover (two tablespoons of salt should do). The next morning, drain them well and spread them evenly on a baking sheet. Toast at 200 degrees while you prepare one pastry shell. Keep close tabs on the pecans—you just want them dry, not scorched. Alternatively, don't soak the pecans. Just toast them for several minutes. They just won't be as smooth or buttery.

Prepare a nine-inch single pie shell and preheat the oven to 350 degrees.

In a medium, heavy saucepan, put four tablespoons of butter, three-quarters of a cup of maple syrup, a pinch of salt, and five large dates, pinched into pieces or chopped. Bring to a simmer over medium heat, whisking intermittently. Remove from heat and whisk in three eggs and either two teaspoons vanilla or a splash of bourbon.

Crumble the nuts into the pie shell. Pour in the filling. Bake until slightly risen and set, but not too firm, about 30 minutes. Let cool for a while before eating.

—R

Strudel

Turks invade Hungary, and the stage is violently set for the remarkable collision of flaky layered pastry (née phyllo) and apples. Five hundred years later, Julie Andrews is singing about brown paper packages and warm apple strudel, under threat of yet another invasion—the Germans. Such a violent past for something so delightful.

As a 16-year-old, I read somewhere (and the legend does appear everywhere strudel is mentioned) that to be properly marriageable, a girl ought to make a strudel dough so thin her fiancé could read the newspaper through it. That doesn't seem unreasonable (provided her fiancé could make a strudel dough so thin she could read passages from Gloria Steinem). Strudel requires plenty of good relationship skills: patience, gentleness, flexibility, and buttery largesse. Unlike puff pastry and croissants, which use exponential functions to multiply their dough layers, every flake in strudel is carefully formed by hand. The strudel goes from a little dough-lump to a transparent sheet of silk, through much cursing and coaxing.

There are some important things to keep in mind when making your tender, eminently elastic dough. First of all, you want to develop the gluten really, really well when you knead it. And then you want to let the gluten rest with a smooth, taut gluten film on top. Second, stretch the dough *carefully*, letting gravity help you out, and watch for snapping, buckling gluten strands, which will later become holes. Finally, stretch the dough impossibly thin. Stretch it so thin it scarcely exists in three dimensions, so thin that it practically disappears altogether and starts floating away toward your towering castles of matrimonial delight in the clouds.

In fact, forget being too careful. Hesitation won't help you any at all. The best stretching will happen when the dough is in the air, not when you're pinching at it on the table.

First, make the dough. Mix together two cups of flour, an egg, a tablespoon of butter or lard, a tablespoon of vinegar, and enough tepid water to make a fairly soft dough. It should seem too sticky. Knead it well, until it becomes elastic and stops sticking to your hands. Fold the edges toward the center and rotate the dough as you go, so that the underside forms a nice, even gluten film. Turn the dough so the smooth film is on top, drape a towel over it, and place a warm bowl upside down over it. Let it rest for an hour.

Throw a clean sheet or other large, finely woven cloth over a table. Dust it with flour, and place the dough lump in the middle. Use a rolling pin to roll it fairly thin, then take the dough in your hands/wrists/forearms and gently stretch it all around. As it gets larger, move around the table to stretch it evenly. Avoid ripping it with your poky little fingers—handle it with your larger, flatter, gentler surfaces. I'm one of those people with coarse, practical hands. To protect the tender dough from my knotty knuckles, I butter the backs of my hands.

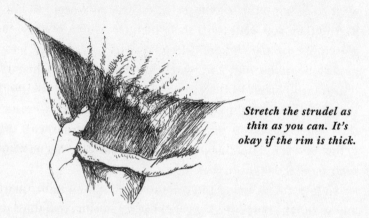

Stretch the strudel as thin as you can. It's okay if the rim is thick.

When it is stretched so thin you can, in fact, see through it, trim off the overhanging thick edges and brush the surface with melted butter or lard. Place your desired filling in a line about two inches away from one edge. Fold that edge up over the filling, then lift the sheet along that edge so the strudel starts rolling down on itself, over and over, stopping when you're about two inches from the opposite side. Fold that edge back over your strudel and tuck the ends.

POPPY SEED FILLING

Poppy seeds are the Central European equivalent of sesame seeds; like sesame, they pair very well with honey, and I don't mean a handful scattered in your muffin. Think poppy seeds in strudel like pecans in pecan pie. If you've ever enjoyed a crumbly bit of halvah, you'll love this crunchy purple filling wrapped in flaky pastry. It is imperative, however, that your poppy seeds be very fresh. They go rancid quite quickly stored at room temperature, and will taste nasty bitter. Buy poppy seeds from a store that restocks them frequently, and store them in the freezer as soon as you bring them home. Frozen, they will keep for the better part of a year.

Traditionally, poppy seeds are crushed in a roller when used in pastry fillings. Try them ground in a coffee grinder (not so fine that they become pasty), or pound them enthusiastically in your mortar and pestle (it's a bit of a trick, what with them being shaped like ball bearings). Or just leave them whole. They're fun to crunch.

Combine one cup of poppy seeds, half cup of milk, quarter cup of honey, one-third cup of chopped raisins, one-third cup of chopped nuts, and a dash of nutmeg in a saucepan. Cook until thickened and remove from heat. Beat an egg with a quarter cup of additional honey and mix into the poppy seeds. Reheat gently, just until simmering again. Turn off the heat and add two tablespoons of butter and a splash of vanilla. Let cool a bit before you use it.

APPLE FILLING

It's the famous way to fill a strudel, and simple enough.

Peel and core four large apples. Chop in medium dice and add four ounces of broken walnuts, two ounces of golden raisins, half cup sugar, one teaspoon cinnamon, and four tablespoons melted butter. Let macerate a bit before you use it.

—R

Sourdough Crepes

Treat your bubbling crock of sour as the old-fashioned convenience food it is. When my crock of sour gets too big, I make a stack of these delicate, flavorful crepes. They work equally well for sweet and savory fillings—for breakfast or for supper.

Put a large skillet over high heat. While it gets hot, whisk together a cup of rye sour (see page 90), four eggs, and a pinch of salt. Gradually add buttermilk or whey (or water or milk) until the batter is soupy—there is a wide range of acceptable consistencies, but the thinner the batter, the more delicate the crepes will be.

When the skillet is quite hot, put a dab of fat in it. Swirl the fat around, then pour a quarter cup of batter in the center of the pan. Immediately lift the skillet, tilt it, and swirl the batter around so it slides out into a circle. Set it back on the heat. In a very short time, the crepe will appear dry on top, and should be golden underneath. Flip it and let it brown lightly on the underside. Start a stack on a plate, covered by a towel. Put a dab of fat in the skillet and make another.

It's much more efficient, of course, to have two or more skillets going at once.

I call these crepes because that's the name most people associate with thin pancakes. They're probably more akin to *pflinzen* or *palacsinta*. Serve them with yogurt, preserves and butter, warm ganache, honey and butter, miso, chutney, dates and cheese, or whatever your favorite flavors are. The type of fat you use makes a big difference, too. Try ghee, bacon drippings, lard, or butter (though be very careful with butter, as it burns at the high heat crepes require).

Shortcakes

Put some whipped cream on slivered strawberries inside a hot, split biscuit and you have a shortcake by the general definition. Technically, "shortcake" refers to a cake with sufficient quantities of fat to shorten the gluten-y properties of flour and render it tender—it's really just another name for "biscuit." Since shortcakes rely on such fresh and few ingredients, select them carefully—homemade baking powder, good, rich cream, and sweet local berries. You simply will not find a good berry in the supermarket unless you like to chomp on shiny tumid hunks of wax. Look for older varieties of strawberries from farms in your area, or pick wild strawberries if they grow near you. The older varieties of strawberries (for example, Chandlers) haven't been bred for storage or size, but for *flavor*. Flavor, of course, is the point of this whole business, but sadly it *isn't* the point of agribusiness. Even mainstream organic strawberries are bred for nothing but appearance and storage—though they do avoid those pesky pesticide residues, which are higher on strawberries than most other fruit, no matter how well you wash them.

Small, modest berries have much more concentrated flavor—especially right at the peak of their ripeness, when they're starting to lose their shine and turn a deep wine red.

THE BAKING POWDER

You can eliminate the bitterness of baking powder if you follow the advice of Edna Lewis, the queen of Southern cookery. She says you ought to make your own. Hush now, it's very simple. In a little jar, put a quarter cup cream of tartar, two tablespoons baking soda, and three tablespoons cornstarch. Mix it with a fork. Use it within a couple of months.

THE SHORTCAKE

A good shortcake is subtly different from a good biscuit. It ought to have just the hint of sweetness, yes, but it also has to soak up a bit of strawberry juiciness, and be soft enough that the berries don't just roll off onto the plate when you try to assemble your cakes. I think cream biscuits do the trick—they're even more delicate than other biscuits. When making other kinds of biscuits, I like to leave the butter chunks fairly large, to create flaky layers. But flaky layers tend to repel the sweet juices of the strawberries, which I want my shortcakes to absorb. So cut the butter fine.

Preheat the oven to 425 degrees.

In a medium bowl, whisk together one and three-quarters cups of flour, half teaspoon of salt, one tablespoon of super-fine sugar, and two tablespoons of homemade baking powder. Cut or rub in half a cup of unsalted butter until the butter pieces are fairly fine—about the consistency of coarse crumbs—but not at all amalgamated with the flour.

Make a well in the middle of the flour and pour in three-quarters cup of cream. The cream can be old, soured cream or half-and-half from the back of your fridge. Such forgotten cream need never go to waste (unless it's full of gross stabilizers and preservatives, yuck). Swiftly stir the dough until it comes together into a single lump. Dump it out on a clean, floured surface and knead it with half a dozen swift strokes. Pat it into a flattish circle and roll it half an inch thick. Cut it with a sharp two- to three-inch biscuit cutter or other round implement, or slice the dough into squares, parallelograms, triangles, or other attractive shapes (not too pointy, or they will burn in the narrow parts). Arrange them on a lightly greased baking sheet and bake until lightly golden, 10 to 15 minutes. Let cool while you whip the cream and prepare the berries. They need to be eaten within the next few hours.

THE FRUIT

Wash a pint of berries and lay them on a towel to dry as you work. Trim off the caps and slice into thin slivers. Sprinkle with a tablespoon or two of sugar and let them yield up their juices while you whip the cream.

You can, of course, make shortcake from any reasonably soft fruit you like. Try raspberries, blackberries, peaches, sweet cherries, or mangoes.

THE CREAM

Look for the richest cream you can buy. Avoid ultra-pasteurized cream, which tastes gummy and flat. Crème fraîche whips up well, too, and is dreamy with strawberries. Whisking by hand makes for lighter cream.

In a medium bowl, whisk a cup of cold, heavy cream with a tablespoon of sugar and a little splash of vanilla. Whisk it and whisk it, beating in as much air as you can, until it gets foamy, then fluffy, and starts to hold its shape. If you beat it too much, it will seize, turn grainy, and eventually become butter. There's no help for seized cream.

THE ASSEMBLY

Split a warm shortcake in half. Put a couple of spoonfuls of strawberries on the bottom half, followed by a dollop of cream. Cap with the top of the shortcake and repeat with the remaining ones.

Just for kicks, put a strawberry sliver and a dollop of cream on top of the composed shortcake.

Doughnuts

Fresh doughnuts fried in real fat are delicate, aromatic pillows quite unrelated to the convenience-store sort. Real doughnuts nearly dissolve, and yet are subtly elastic. They have a clean flavor and texture—no grease from gummed-up oils or that waxy hydrogenated mouthfeel. Yes, I use lard. Take warning: Most commercial lard has been partially hydrogenated to extend its shelf life. Instead, render your own (see Rendering Fat, page 100), or find some from a quality source. Check the label. A good butcher should either stock ready-made lard, or point you in the right direction.

Vegetarians, use ghee for frying your doughnuts. It has a high smoke point and makes a much better product than oil of any sort.

This is a traditional Pennsylvania German potato doughnut, using the same sort of dough that is used for making *fastnachts* on the Tuesday before Lent. Potatoes lighten and tenderize the dough.

A WORD ON FLOUR

My mother uses whole-wheat flour for six cups of the flour in this recipe, and all-purpose for the rest. Her doughnuts are delicious and almost wholesome. For the most tender doughnuts, use just all-purpose flour (or a blend of pastry flour and bread flour). Bread flour on its own is too strong and makes an unnecessarily sturdy doughnut. Take your pick.

MAKING DOUGH

Either in the morning or the night before, make plain mashed potatoes. One pound of russet potatoes will do the trick quite well, but the little reds and Yukon golds are wonderfully waxy. Don't worry about all the fancy mashed potato things you could do: just peel, roughly cube, and boil those potatoes. Drain off the cooking water when they're soft and mash them thoroughly. You need two cups mashed potatoes. If you like, you can reduce the yeast to one and a half teaspoons, make your dough the night before, and let it rise in a cool spot overnight.

Dissolve two tablespoons dry yeast in a cup of lukewarm water and set it aside. Scald a quart of milk: Bring it slowly to the steaming point on low heat, stirring all the while. Remove it from the heat and mix it in a large bowl with the two cups of mashed potatoes, one cup of butter, and one cup of sugar (or half a cup of honey). Let this mixture cool to lukewarm before adding the yeast and six cups of flour, stir it well, and let it sit again until the yeast makes it all foam up—20 minutes or so.

Stir in two beaten eggs, one tablespoon of salt, and eight cups of flour. Check the consistency. You want the dough to be soft but firm enough to knead. Depending on what sort of flour you've used, the dough may be stiff enough at this point—or you may need as much as an additional quart. Add it, stirring in each cup until it's stiff enough that you must knead it by hand.

Clean off your hands, flour a clean tabletop, transfer the dough to the tabletop, and knead it. Add flour as you work if the dough is too sticky, but resist the temptation to add flour every time the dough adheres a wee bit to your hands. The potatoes, fat, and milk will make the dough much softer and glossier than regular bread doughs. After 10 minutes of kneading, the dough will become lustrous and supple, and small blisters will even appear on the surface. Return it to a large buttered bowl, cover it with a tea towel, and let it rise until double, which may take a couple of hours or more if the room is cool.

SHAPING THE DOUGH

Gently knead the dough to deflate it, divide it into four portions, and let it rest for a few minutes while you make sure everything is in order. You'll want a large, lightly floured surface for rolling out the dough, a sharp knife or doughnut cutter, lightly floured sheet trays to put the cut doughnuts on, and tea towels to keep the rising doughnuts from drying out.

Take a portion of the dough and roll it out, sprinkling flour under and on top of the dough to keep it from sticking as you go. Aim to get it fairly even and about three-quarters of an inch thick. It will want to retract and thicken up, so you may need to roll it slightly thinner.

If you have a doughnut cutter, flour it lightly and cut out your doughnuts. Put the holes and scraps in a pile to be rerolled. You can also use a biscuit cutter three to four inches in diameter, and just cut a slit in the middle for the hole. The hole doesn't need to be very large, and the doughnuts will in fact look much puffier if it isn't. If you don't happen to have a specialized doughnut cutter or an intense need for roundness, I recommend making rectangular doughnuts (*fastnachts*). You'll have hardly any scraps to reroll and square-edged doughnuts are rather stunning to look at. Using a large, sharp knife, cut the dough into three-inch strips, and then make four-inch cuts the other direction. Cut a one-inch slit in the middle of the doughnut. Yes, the sizing is somewhat important—if the doughnuts are too large, they'll get too dark on the outside before the inside is done. The slit or hole in the middle helps the insides cook evenly.

Transfer the cut doughnuts to the floured trays and cover them before rolling out the next portion of the dough. When all the doughnuts are shaped, let them rise. This time, you don't want them to double in height quite all the way, or they'll be too tender and deflate when they hit the hot fat. It shouldn't take much more than an hour, and by the time you finish cutting, the first doughnuts you shaped will be well on their way.

THE GLAZE

You can make your glaze while the doughnuts rise, or a day in advance. A simple mixture of two cups of sugar and several tablespoons of cinnamon is perfectly delicious, but sticky, glossy glazes are really appealing, too. What I don't recommend are intense, heavy glazes like chocolate or caramel, which mask the homemade delicacy of your doughnuts. See glaze recipes below.

FRYING THE DOUGHNUTS

In a large, deep, heavy-bottomed pot, heat enough lard or ghee to be at least four inches deep when melted. You may watch its progress with a thermometer—between 350 and 375 degrees is your perfect doughnut temperature. Add a piece of dough if you want to check its progress. At the right temperature, the dough will sizzle and sizzle, puff rapidly, and turn a nice light golden color within a few minutes. Of course, as soon as you add a lot of doughnuts, the fat will cool down a bit, so you may want to heat it a little bit more than necessary.

Place a metal cooling rack over a sheet tray on a surface near the stove for draining the doughnuts when they're done. Being cautious about hot fat spattering, slide four or five risen doughnuts into the fat—as many as will fit without crowding. They'll rise to the surface as they cook. Let them fry, flipping them partway through, until lightly golden. Remove to the rack and fry the next round of doughnuts.

GLAZING

While the doughnuts are still hot, but after they've drained a bit, dip them in your glaze of choice and let them drain again. You can hang them on a spoon over the glaze bowl, or put them back on the rack. Leftover glaze keeps quite well in the fridge.

BASIC GLAZE

Mash a tablespoon of butter into a pound of powdered sugar. Beat in one teaspoon of vanilla and a quarter cup of cream. Add more cream—a tiny bit at a time—if it seems too thick.

Variations: Try adding your favorite citrus zest and using its juice instead of cream. Or substitute a couple of tablespoons of a delicious liqueur for part of the cream. Or add a drop of almond or other extract. A grating of mace or nutmeg is nice.

MAPLE OR HONEY GLAZE

Melt half a cup of butter and whisk in a quarter cup of maple syrup (or honey) and two tablespoons of cream. Add half a cup of powdered sugar and whisk until smooth. Let cool for a bit to thicken. If it gets too thick, reheat it gently.

—R

Bourbon Truffles

I've had enough of rum and brandy and schnappsy, schmaltzy saccharine confections. It's whiskey as tickles my likerous fancy, and it's whiskey as I'll lace my chocolate with.

Buy a bottle of smooth bourbon, or go snooping behind your housemates' beds and dressers to find that old bottle of Maker's or Bulleit. Then go buy a large chunk of very dark chocolate (70 percent or more). Cube half of it and melt it gently in a double boiler with an equal amount of butter. Remove from the heat before it's all melted and stir it till butter and chocolate have formed a lustrous union of liquid delight (aka ganache). Whisk in whiskey to taste. It ought to put a little warmth in your tummy: the goal is to make a truffle that melts the whole way down.

Chill the ganache till firm enough to mold into little truffle-size balls. Chill the balls while you chop the remaining half of the chocolate and place it in the double boiler, reserving several sizeable chunks for later. Stir the chocolate as it melts, remove from the heat before it's all liquid, and when it's just barely there, add the reserved chunks. Let the chunks cool it down and when they have melted clean away, take the first bourbon ball and drop it in the melted chocolate. Swish it around with a fork, lift the ball on the tines of the fork, and tap it a bit so the excess chocolate drips off. Slide the truffle onto a tray. It should set up glossy and firm, if the temper is right. If the chocolate loses its temper, just add more chocolate chunks, allowing the new chocolate to melt in slowly and infect the distempered chocolate with its correct crystalline structure.

It's not any more sinful than fruitcake, right? And if you happen to greet the sunrise with a nice truffle, or three, it surely couldn't be called whiskey before breakfast, could it? And if you keep a little baggie of bourbon bonbons in your purse for those tedious PTA meetings, that doesn't make you a lush, does it now?

—R

Dutch Baby

As a girl, I used to wake up on a Saturday morning and make a Dutch Baby. A friend and I would play wholesome educational board games while it baked, counting every minute with growling tummies.

When finally the Dutch Baby emerged, towering, glistening, and golden with butter, we smothered it with jams and syrups and devoured it alone in one sitting. We analyzed the different varieties of butter-crispies that formed in its eggy strata and bragged about our insatiable adolescent appetites—after which we ran barefoot in the woods, hunting wild mushrooms.

It's basically a sweet version of a Yorkshire pudding.

Melt a stick of butter in a large cast-iron skillet—either in the oven while it preheats to 425 degrees, or on the stovetop. In another bowl, whisk together four room-temperature eggs, one cup all-purpose flour, one cup milk, and half cup sugar (brown is nice, especially if you sprinkle the babies with cinnamon). Pour the batter into the melted butter and pop it in the oven for something like 20 to 25 minutes. Set the table and put out maple syrup, honey, marmalades, and yogurt.

When it's puffed and golden, get everyone to the table and serve it with a flourish. Its glory is fleeting.

—R

Bibliography

Bertolli, Paul. *Cooking by Hand*. New York: Clarkson Potter, 2003.

David, Elizabeth. *English Bread and Yeast Cookery*. New York: Viking, 1980.

Fallon, Sally. *Nourishing Traditions*. Washington, DC: New Trends Publishing Inc., 2001.

Grigson, Jane. *Charcuterie and French Pork Cookery*. Harmondsworth: Penguin, 1970.

Grigson, Jane. *Good Things*. New York: Athenaeum, 1984.

Hamelman, Jeffrey. *Bread: A Baker's Book of Techniques and Recipes*. Hoboken, NJ: John Wiley and Sons, 2004.

Jenkins, Nancy Harmon. *The Essential Mediterranean*. New York: William Morrow, 2003.

Kander, Mrs. Simon. *The Settlement Cookbook*. Milwaukee, WI: The Settlement Cook Book Co., 1951.

Katz, Sandor Ellix. *Wild Fermentation*. White River Junction, VT: Chelsea Green, 2003.

Kutas, Rytek. *Great Sausage Making and Meat Curing*. Buffalo, NY: MacMillan, 2007.

Lewis, Edna. *In Pursuit of Flavor*. New York: Alfred A. Knopf, 1988.

Longacre, Doris Janzen. *More-with-Less Cookbook*. Scottdale, PA: Herald Press, 1976.

Marianski, Stanley. *The Art of Making Fermented Sausages*. Parker, CO: Outskirts Press, 2008.

McGee, Harold. *On Food and Cooking: The Science and Lore of the Kitchen*. New York: Scribner, 2004.

Merritt, Fannie Farmer. *The Boston Cooking-School Cookbook*. Boston, MA: Little, Brown and Company, 1942.

Reinhart, Peter, and Ron Manville. *The Bread Baker's Apprentice*. Berkeley, CA: Ten Speed Press, 2001.

Ruhlmann, Michael, and Brian Polcyn. *Charcuterie*. New York: W. W. Norton, 2005.

Showalter, Mary Emma. *Mennonite Community Cookbook*. Scottdale, PA.: The Mennonite Community Association, 1957.

Shurtleff, William, and Akiko Aoyagi. *The Book of Miso*, 2nd Edition. Berkeley, CA: Ten Speed Press, 2001.

Silverton, Nancy. *Breads from La Brea Bakery*. New York: Villard, 1996.

Sources

G.E.M. CULTURES

www.gemcultures.com

Supplies *koji* spores, sourdough starters, and dairy cultures

AIRLOCKS, BREWING EQUIPMENT

www.rebelbrewer.com

www.benshomebrew.com

RAW MILK

www.realmilk.com/where.html

THE SAUSAGE MAKER INC.

www.sausagemaker.com

NEW ENGLAND CHEESEMAKING SUPPLY CO.

www.cheesemaking.com

Acknowledgments

First, we would like to thank Danielle Svetcov, through whom we first met over a cookbook about constipation. And thanks to Monica Verma, our fabulous agent, and the indefatigable Maria Gagliano at Perigee.

Ken's personal thanks go to Kristina Nies for hooking me up with Twamley on cheese. To Krishnendu Ray, thanks for unwittingly suggesting the name Durga for a sourdough starter. Thanks to Podesto's grocery, which supplied me with nearly everything I cooked for this book. Thanks to Meg Ragland for helping me smear a rabbit. Christine Eagle proved a perfect partner in crime, nay a goddess of game, on so many occasions, with a whole deer, a bear, and a little piggie. And thanks to Abecca and Christine for a lovely day of cheese-making. To my hoodies—Ustachs, Qualls, Burr/Siegels, Heagleys, Cooperman/Maxwells, and everyone who has shown up to join in the hallowed repast and revelry. And I must thank my dear friends on the ASFS Listserv, who bore with remarkable patience the tedious string of questions and comments that issued from the experiments connected with writing this book, as well as my fellow blogsters who helped with comments—especially Peter

Hertzmann, for his wicked conversion charts. Sadly, the blog in its incarnation as thinkpad for this book had to be euthanized for copyright purposes.

Rosanna's thanks go first to David Henry Sterry, whose workshop on writing I sneaked into, and who agreed to meet with me, heard my tale, and sent me to Danielle Svetcov. Thanks to all the housemates who've had to share tiny kitchens with me and all my mold and crocks and pastry scraps—Avy, Marina, Mike the Russian, Val, Louisa, Ken, Anna, and Joe. Thanks to Mariza Ruvalcaba for my introduction to south-of-the-border cookery. Thanks to Norah Hoover for the photo shoot. Thanks to Papa for making all that maple syrup and hunting all those deer. Thanks to Mama for drawing all the illustrations—and for letting me bake bread instead of mowing the lawn! And of course, thanks to William Crawford Henderson, who fed my sourdough starter when I was tired, built my blog and bicycle, and put the kettle on.

THE END.

Index

About the Authors

PHOTO BY BENJAMIN ALBALA

KEN ALBALA is professor of history at the University of the Pacific in Stockton, California, where he teaches courses on the Renaissance and Reformation, Food History, and the History of Medicine. He is the author of many books on food, including *Eating Right in the Renaissance, Food in Early Modern Europe, Cooking in Europe 1250–1650, The Banquet: Dining in the Great Courts of Late Renaissance Europe, Beans: A History* (winner of the 2008 International Association of Culinary Professionals Jane Grigson Award), *Pancake*, and the forthcoming *World Cuisines* written with the Culinary Institute of America. He is also the editor of three food series for Greenwood Press with 27 volumes in print and is now editing a four-volume *Food Cultures of the World Encyclopedia*. Albala has been the book reviews editor of *Food Culture and Society* for the past six years and is now coeditor of the journal. He is currently researching a history of theological controversies surrounding fasting in the Reformation Era and editing two collected volumes of essays, one on the Renaissance, the other on food and faith.

PHOTO BY NORA HOOVER

ROSANNA NAFZIGER grew up on a mountain in West Virginia. She spent her girlhood working in the orchard, planting beans, and selling pies at the farmers' market. Now she translates the traditions of her Appalachian Mennonite upbringing to the urban kitchen on her blog, Paprikahead.com. A chef, nanny, and editor, she lives in San Francisco. This is her first book.